HISTORICAL RECORD
SOCIETY

ISBN 0 85155 035 5

Key to Railways proposed but not built 1844–1910

————————— 1844–1846

— — — — — — —· 1852–1864

—·—·—·—·—·— 1865–1910

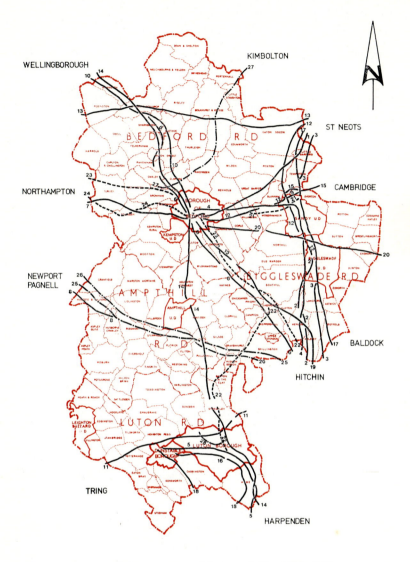

Railways proposed but not built   1844 – 1910

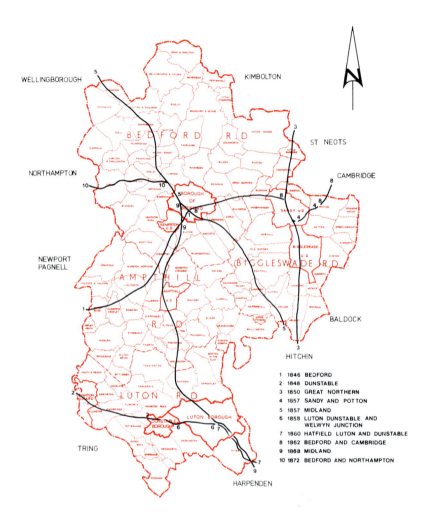

Map of lines constructed   1846 – 1872

THE PUBLICATIONS OF THE BEDFORDSHIRE
HISTORICAL RECORD SOCIETY
VOLUME 53

THE RAILWAY AGE
IN BEDFORDSHIRE

F. G. COCKMAN

PUBLISHED BY THE SOCIETY   ·   1974

CONTENTS

ILLUSTRATIONS (*between pages 64 and 65*)

PLANS (*on frontispiece*)

Plans and illustrations. The two plans were drawn by the County Planning Department. The illustrations are reproduced by kind permission of Mr F. Banfield (14); Bedford Museum (1); Bedfordshire County Record Office (4, 6, 15); British Rail (5); Mr J. W. Brown (11); Mr F. G. Cockman (8); Holland Press (13); Luton Museum (2, 3, 7, 10, 12); Mr A. G. Underwood (9).

INTRODUCTION

Anyone studying the social history of this country cannot fail to be amazed at the change which took place during the 19th century in modes of travel. This change was remarkable not only for the great increase in speed, but also for its suddenness. As travel became easier and cheaper, it became more common. One cause was the adaptation of steam to locomotion which began early in the century. Although pioneers like Blenkinsop, Hackworth and Hedley had done much useful work, it is George Stephenson who assists us in remembering the date, by naming one of his engines 'Blucher'. Another cause was the formation of Corporate Societies or Joint Stock Companies who could command sufficient capital to undertake the building of the new railroads. In this country the old established systems of transport by road and canal quickly fell victims to the steam operated railway because it matched the canal for dependability and beat the road for speed. The following chapters will endeavour to show how the railways attained a high standard of public service after the many initial mistakes which are all too easily condemned by hindsight. The country came to rely on its trains, and, while the railways prospered, the public was never let down. In fact the nation, when once it had abandoned its peripatetic habits and had taken to the flanged wheel on steel rail, became travel conscious and so stepped easily into the petrol age when it arrived.

This book deals with the impact made by railways on Victorian society in Bedfordshire. A suitable date for the commencement is the year 1846 when the Bedford Railway was opened – the county's first line, and I have chosen 1890 or thereabouts for the closing date of the narrative. By 1890 the railways were just beginning to respond to the outstanding 'Regulation of Railways Act, 1889', probably the most important act since Gladstone's of 1844. The 1889 Act brought our railways up to a pitch of safety, comfort and efficiency which could not be matched anywhere else in the world.

In chapter 7 I have mentioned briefly the Bedfordshire lines that were planned, but not proceeded with. These are dealt with in much more detail in my typescript account 'Bedfordshire Railways planned but not built' which can be consulted at the County Record Office. When I was writing this Miss Bell, the County Archivist, suggested that I should tackle the question of the social effects on the county of the coming of the railways. I have drawn heavily on the documents in the County Record Office, and here I can pay tribute to the willing help of the County Record Office staff. I have also had massive help from the Public Record Office, where again the staff are ever ready to assist. The writing of this work has been a great enjoyment, and I hope that some readers will both enjoy reading it, and find the contents instructive.

Bedford 1969   F. G. COCKMAN

SOURCES

It has not been thought necessary to give a separate reference for every individual document quoted in the text. Most documents are among those deposited at the Bedfordshire County Record Office, the main source being the Woburn estate correspondence deposited by the Trustees of the Bedford Settled Estate (R 3). Other documents are the diary of Catherine Young (later Maclear) chapters 1 and 2 (AD 1719); letters to the Clerk of the Peace chapters 1 and 7 (Q.S.R.); the Great Northern Railway's valuer's correspondence chapter 3 (RR 3 and RR 8); Dr Jacob Mountain's letters chapter 5 (X 67/581–7); Bute estate correspondence chapter 5 (G/DDA); Bedfordshire Quarter Sessions Minutes chapters 9, 10 and 14 (Q.S.M.); Bedford General Infirmary Minutes chapter 9 (HO: B/M); Coroner's Register chapter 9 and appendix (CO 11); letter concerning the Leighton Buzzard Enclosure Award Text chapter 10 (BO 1868); the Williamson diaries chapter 10 (M 3/5) and the Brooks diaries in the same chapter (LL 17/281); the Luton petition chapter 13 (Q.G.E.); the Wythes investment book chapter 14 (X 98/7).

The Wade-Gery letters quoted in chapters 10 and 11 are in the possession of Mrs W. R. Wade-Gery; the Midland Railway Board's minutes and company correspondence in chapter 4 are now at the Public Record Office.

Newspaper reports generally come from either the *Bedfordshire Times and Independent* or the *Bedfordshire Mercury*, but of other newspapers the *Railway Times* and *Herapath's Railway Journal* have been most used.

As regards printed secondary sources, I have relied most heavily on *British Railway History* by C. Hamilton Ellis and *The Railway Mania* by H. Grote Lewin.

CHAPTER 1

BEFORE THE RAILWAYS

If we agree with Pope that the proper study of mankind is man, then we cannot fail to be curious about the methods employed by man to travel. Progress in methods of travel not only saved effort but helped to increase wealth, as Lord Bacon saw when he said 'Truly there are three things which make a nation great and prosperous – fertile soil, busy workshops and easy conveyance for men and commodities from one place to another'. Before the railway era transport in Great Britain depended either on water, which meant canals or rivers, or on land, which implied packhorses or wheeled traffic on inferior roads. Roads preceded the canals, but it will be more convenient to deal with canals first.

Rivers have always provided a cheap form of transport, but can be affected by floods or, conversely, can dry up. It was to obtain something more dependable that Francis, 3rd Duke of Bridgewater began, in the 18th century, to construct that system of canals which bears his name. He obtained a private Act of Parliament and secured the services of a capable engineer – James Brindley. Commencing at Worsley, near Manchester, the canals proved a success, and the system spread over the country. Brindley showed his ability by taking the Bridgewater canal over the Barton aqueduct – a forerunner of the great railway structures which we see today. On the rivers, barges and wherries had to depend on the wind for power, and it was a great step forward when towpaths were laid down alongside the canals permitting the more reliable horse power to be used. It is not surprising, therefore, to read that the canal mileage increased from 1,500 to 5,000 between 1760 and 1830. If we believe that history repeats itself, we shall not be too amazed to learn that there was a 'Canal Mania' in 1794 when twenty new canal schemes costing £3 million received Parliamentary sanction. The construction of these inland waterways required armies of workmen and for the first time we read of the 'navigators' as the men were called. The name was soon shortened to 'navvies' and they numbered in their ranks many Irish and continental workers. It must have given the British public little consolation in 1846 to know that it had all happened before, and when we read of the happenings in 1794 and after, the familiar phrases occur – 'beef and beer', 'poaching of game', 'attacks on prisons' and other disturbances of the peace. The canal promoters, like the railwaymen who followed, had to contend with shortage of labour, expensive legislation and excessive compensation for landowners.

The canals soon began to affect the life of the country. They had a great appeal to manufacturers of fragile goods because of the smooth transit – for example in the Potteries. Nearer home, the Duke of Bedford made great use of the Grand Junction canal at Leighton Buzzard. But the great prosperity of the canals was obtained at the expense of other means of transport. The owners of packhorses suffered a severe loss, and the canal companies paid enormous dividends – far larger than the greatest declared by the railways. The inland waterways made their great contribution to the prosperity of the country when they had only the waggon as a competitor. They had one great weakness – their leisurely pace. This was at best the walking speed of the horse, but it suffered when there were many locks to negotiate. When another means of communication arose, it was a case of the survival of the fastest. The canal boats' fate was shared by the stage and mail coaches.

Travel overland by coach was so expensive that only the wealthier classes could indulge in it, and it was also slow. A schoolmaster named Pennant went from Chester to London in 1739 by stagecoach and took six days to reach the capital. The Edinburgh coach took nine days on the journey to London, carrying six passengers inside and nine outside. The fare of £7 (single journey) must have been far exceeded by the cost of putting up each night at an inn. An alternative for a poor man was to go by stage waggon with wheels 14 in wide sending up dust clouds in dry weather; or if you were rich you could hire a postchaise, which would whisk you to Edinburgh in 36 hours at a cost of £70.

At the turn of the century, Telford with his new gravel roads and Macadam who laid down the modern metalled surface, had so improved stage coach travel that a great industry sprang up. Early in the 19th century it was estimated that there were 3,300 stagecoaches in existence, with an army of 30,000 drivers, guards, ostlers and horse keepers at the various stages, driving and tending the 150,000 horses required to maintain the services. The cost per mile in England was 4d or 5d – a large sum at that time – but the coaching service was fulfilling a public need and it was a safe way to travel. Despite the improvement in the road surfaces and the changing of horses every 12 miles or so, the speed of the stage coach was low – about 9 m.p.h. average. The low speed kept down casualties and on the average only three passengers a year were killed on the road. The coaches and the canal narrow boats were complementary rather than competitive. The former carried passengers and parcels; the latter took manufactured goods to the ports and carried coal from the north. Agricultural produce also went by canal.

In 1832, fourteen years before Bedford saw its first railway, Catherine Young wrote in her diary that she had left Haverfordwest by the night mail coach and had arrived in Oxford at 11.30 p.m. next day. She left Oxford at 7 a.m. on the morning following, and arrived in Bedford at 3 p.m. Her route had been via Carmarthen, Brecon, Monmouth and Gloucester. A letter which she sent on 28th July 1832 required a stamp of 1s. In 1833 Mrs Young left Bedford for London at 8.30 in the morning by the 'Times' coach 'and arrived in Bernard Street before dinner'. When in 1834 she left London by the Kettering coach, arriving in Bedford at 3 p.m., she says 'Very tired'. The journey from Cambridge to Bedford was also slow, as we see from a letter from J. D. Fitch to Theed Pearse, Clerk of the Peace, in 1843 – 'Our coaches to Bedford from Cambridge leave at 7.30 a.m., and arrive at 10.30. Will you say whether I shall be in time for the commencement of the Appeal Business?'

Public opinion is clearly shown by a statement from the wool merchants of Yorkshire in 1844, who in support of the Leeds & Bradford Railway said 'It costs as much to bring wool by waggon from Leeds to Bradford, 10 miles, as from Hull to Leeds, 58 miles by rail'. Bedford had been served by a large number of daily coaches going to all points of the compass. When the London and Birmingham Railway was opened in 1838 many coaches were taken off. One of the last to survive was the Bedford 'Times' coach, but it survived only a week after the Bedford Railway had commenced its operations on 17th November 1846.

Needing faster, cheaper and more reliable transport, the country had taken to the railways. The great railway age had arrived.

CHAPTER 2

THE FIRST THREE LINES: LONDON & BIRMINGHAM; BEDFORD; DUNSTABLE

The Liverpool & Manchester Railway, opened 1830, showed the way England was to go. The Stockton & Darlington Railway had indeed been in operation for five years, but it was still chiefly a mineral line, and now it was the turn of the big cities. Manchester needed faster transport to bring in the cotton and to take out the manufactured goods. Liverpool was a port with an increasing capacity for shipping; a railway connecting the two was an obvious necessity. The interests of the big cities could be served by (to quote L. T. C. Rolt) 'Self-propelled vehicles of great weight covering long distances at high speed on rail-prescribed courses'. The business-houses of London wished to be connected with the ports of Bristol and Southampton and with the manufacturing centre of Birmingham. Thus by 1833, the two Rennies and Robert Stephenson had surveyed rival routes between London and Birmingham and were waiting the decision of the Board of Directors. The Board cautiously engaged another engineer of repute, J. U. Rastrick (who later built the London & Brighton Railway) to give his opinion on the two proposed routes, and he eulogised Stephenson's by saying 'Let nothing deter you from executing the work in the most substantial manner and on the most scientific principles so that it may serve as a model for all future railways and become the wonder and admiration of Posterity'.

Later in the same year Robert Stephenson staked out the route, and before the first train ran, five years later, he was to walk the distance between London and Birmingham fourteen times. The first turf was cut near Chalk Farm in 1834 and the railway is of particular interest to Bedfordshire because it came so close (its station just across the border in Linslade was called Leighton Buzzard) and the branches it threw off from Bletchley in 1846 and Leighton Buzzard in 1848 were the first lines to serve this county.

It cost the company £500,000 just to get their bill through Parliament and to buy off opposition, and work all along the line started in 1835, employing 20,000 men. Such a vast number of navvies made a great impact on the peaceful countryside, and one of the worst affected villages was Kilsby where the great tunnel was made. In the end the villagers rose against the 'invaders' to cure the worst abuses. Another battle was fought at Wolverton where Stephenson wished to bridge the Grand Junction canal. The bridge was built at Christmas when the canal men were enjoying themselves elsewhere, but the structure was torn down on discovery. However, the railwaymen triumphed when the Court of Chancery granted an injunction against the canal owners. When this part of the line was under construction Robert Stephenson used to stay at the *Cock Inn*, Stony Stratford.

Landowners were in a peculiar position; they might oppose railways from fear of despoliation of the amenities of their estates, or they might invest heavily in the company and welcome the line. Furthermore, there was always the possibility of making some profit by selling materials to the contractors, as we see from this letter to E. Crocker, the Duke of Bedford's Steward at Woburn, from W. G. Adam, the Agent-in-Chief in London, dated 27th November 1835:

'The Duke asked me today whether I had heard of the great demand for timber which the Birmingham Railway had created – that he understood they bought all sorts at a very liberal price and desired me to write to you to say that he thought you should take Ireland through the Woods etc, and see whether this demand could not be made the means of clearing the woods and selling what might not go off readily in other ways.

'I said that we had had some communication about the Railway – but that I did not understand that it was to such an extent. It appears that the Duke speaks from Lord Holland's information and he from Swaffield. And if I understand correctly Swaffield had been dealing. At all events the Duke seemed to think that this was an opportunity. Will you therefore make further enquiry so as to be able to satisfy his Grace and examine the wood carefully with Ireland to see whether you can make any sales particularly of inferior articles.'

The London & Birmingham attracted the attention of the artist J. C. Bourne, who spent day after day watching the engineers at work and sketching their achievements. His pictures were at the Museum of Transport at Clapham. By 1838 the railway was almost ready for opening – except for the dread Kilsby tunnel which had ruined contractors through its hidden quantities of sand and water. Until this great tunnel was completed, trains ran from Euston to Denbigh Hall, just north of Bletchley, where passengers alighted and travelled to Rugby by horse-drawn coach. Here they re-entered a train and proceeded to Birmingham. Robert Stephenson took over the tunnel works, and by 17th September the line was opened throughout from London to Birmingham (Curzon Street). The Leon family, who owned Bletchley Park, have recorded all this in a plaque in the railway bridge which crosses Watling Street near Bletchley. The site of Denbigh Hall was commemorated by an inn on the road and by a signal box on the railway. Both have now gone.

The great works at Kilsby and Roade had increased the cost of the line from the estimated £2,400,000 to £5,500,000, and although this was a burden to the shareholders, the greatest price was paid by Robert Stephenson, whose health was undermined by five years' mental and physical strain.

From September 1838 then, the inhabitants of south-west Bedfordshire could count themselves fortunate as having access to one of the great trunk routes of the country, and Leighton Buzzard station was well patronised from the first. The townsmen of Bedford however were less content as they had to make their own way to the station known as Bletchley and Fenny Stratford, sixteen miles distant. To add to their discomfiture, neighbouring county towns were already enjoying the new mode of travel, for the Northern & Eastern Railway had reached Hertford in 1843 by means of a branch line from Broxbourne, and the same company (now leased to the Eastern Counties Railway) began to serve Cambridge as from July 1845.

It was only to be expected, therefore, that local tradesmen were anxious to form a company to construct a railway to serve Bedford by a branch from the nearest main line. They therefore looked to the London & Birmingham, as a branch line to Bletchley would be only 16 miles in length. As the railway was to run through the estates of the Duke of Bedford he was actively involved. Thus the Bedford Railway Company was formed in 1845 with Theed Pearse junior as Secretary, the capital being £125,000.

This letter from T. Bennett (the Duke of Bedford's Steward at Woburn) to C. Haedy (the Duke's Agent-in-Chief in London) dated 22nd July 1840, shows that the idea was already in the air five years earlier. Elger was a Bedford builder.

'I met with Mr. Elger today at Bedford, and had some conversation with him as to this being a good time for selling Building Ground in Bedford or not . . . Mr. Elger says that should the Railway go on, it is impossible to say what alteration may take place in the value of property in the Town; and upon the whole . . . he thinks that persons who can hold their property should not bring it into Market just at this time.

'There was a meeting held yesterday about the Railway, and the project was most favourably entertained by the Meeting. Mr. Whitbread advocates it most strenuously, and will offer every support he can to it, and so also do many other proprietors on or about the Line. I think that if the Manchester people make up their minds that a second line of rail is required, they will carry it, and if Bedford does not take advantage of the Line, some other Town probably will.

'Northampton at this time is a deplorable instance of refusing to have a great Line passing through or near a Town. They are just as much shut out from the great thoroughfare as Woburn is – with this difference, that Northampton might have had it and did not see the advantage, and now they would give anything to get it when they cannot.'

The reference to Northampton is interesting. The London & Birmingham line missed Northampton, and this was due to the energetic tactics of the Duke of Grafton and Sir William Wake. It was this damaging form of obstruction that Bennett was anxious to avoid. Four years later, the wave of speculation known as the Railway Mania was just beginning and several schemes affected Bedfordshire. Bennett refers to some of these in his letter to Haedy dated 12th May 1844:

'Bedford was quite alive yesterday about Railways – it appears the Birmingham people are determined on a branch from Bletchley (near Fenny Stratford) to Bedford, the Terminus about the Infirmary, [for which] the late Mr. Gotobed's field or one of the Duke's will probably be chosen. The line then proceeds through Kempston, Wootton, Marston, Lidlington, tunnel through Brogborough Hill, come out about Holcut, over the lower part of Aspley to Wavendon and Sympson and Bletchley.

'The Northern line are also surveying from Bedford, Terminus to be near the House of Industry, to cross at Goldington to Cople Meadows past Willington Manor House and Church in a direct line to meet the Rail at Girtford. Then the Direct London & Manchester people are again in the field by St. Albans, Luton, Bedford etc. This line touches upon the Duke's Estate at Maulden, St. Leonards, at the end of Oakley on the Clapham side, then again at Souldrop – so if they all go on we shall have Railways as common as Turnpike roads.'

The letter refers to three railways. The first is the Bedford railway which in the event did not tunnel under Brogborough but went further south; the Great Northern did not in the end build their Bedford branch, and the Direct London & Manchester was never constructed.

The decision of the Board of the Bedford Railway to choose a route south of that originally planned is recorded in a letter from Bennett to Haedy on 8th August 1844:

'The line for the Bedford–Bletchley Rail is now set out to Brogborough Hill from Bedford to the Duke's Lidlington Estate. It is most objectionable, and one which I think should be most strenuously opposed by his Grace, for I cannot see any advantage any other part of the property will get to compensate for the way in which Lidlington Great farm will be cut up. Instead of taking a direct line from Bedford they go south to the race meadow and keep on that (the southern) side of the vale, considerably to the south of Marston church, and in Lidlington village nearly touch upon Mr. Thomas' rick yard. By this line I presume they get more easily through Brogborough Hill, but they pass through much more valuable land almost all the way. I suspect this circuitous line is in some measure to get away from Mr. Littledale who has built a large house [at Kempston] and Mr. Stewart who is building now, but this latter ought not to weigh with them because Mr. S. had not commenced building when the line was projected. Whatever their object may be, I think some means should be taken to ascertain if the present line is what they intend to apply to Parliament for.'

The real reason was, of course, that it was much cheaper to take the line through a deep cutting to the south than to bore a tunnel through the hill to the north. That the owners of land stood to gain by the coming of the railway is borne out by another letter from Bennett to Haedy written on 6th December 1844, which deals also with a proposed Ely to Bedford Railway.

'Mr. Pearse said this would make a wonderful change in the value of the riverside property at Bedford, but even the Bletchley line will do this, and that the Bedford merchants to spite the navigation are promoting the Bletchley line most strenuously without forseeing the effect.

'Evidently this allusion was, that the terminus being at St. Leonards, the Depot for Coals and Merchandise coming from the Birmingham line, will naturally be formed there, and that will become the business part of the town for what is now done at the Riverside. It is true they are to have a main way from the terminus to the River, but it will not answer to put the Coals in boats to carry down a few hundred yards and then to carry them on their wharfs. The labour of this will beat them, so will carting from the Rail to their wharf. If the Ely line goes on, then all carriage both from the east and west must centre there so that the St. Leonards property has the prospect of being immensely improved in value. Mr. Gotobed's field will be required for these purposes also.'

Although the Ely line was not constructed, St Leonards (the present St John's station) became a business centre as forecast by Bennett. He refers again to the Bletchley line when writing to Haedy on 24th January 1845:

> 'I understand the Ely & Bedford people have abandoned their projected line to Bedford, and intend only to try and get one to Huntingdon . . . and before the Bletchley Line is too far advanced, it strikes me that the Duke should ask them . . . to give some proper assurance that they will give us a station either in the parish of Ridgmont, Crawley or Aspley . . .'

Meanwhile the Duchess of Bedford had performed the ceremony of cutting the first sod, approximately at the half-way point, Husborne Crawley. The customary silver spade was used and a wheelbarrow made from oak grown on the Bedford estate. Writing to Haedy from Park Farm Office on 12th November 1845 Bennett once more shows his interest in land values:

> 'I think that they are so anxious to get possession, [that] the landowners may rather dictate their own terms as to payment than submit to the dictation of the Company. All public bodies are disposed to carry things with a high hand, and the only way is to keep them out of possession until we are satisfied.'

The following letter from Bennett to Haedy dated 21st November 1845 is interesting because of the local people mentioned, for example, Mr Swaffield, the founder of the well-known firm of estate agents in Ampthill. Bennett also refers to the branch to the river and to the extension of the Bedford railway to Cambridge, surveyed by Robert Stephenson in 1845, and rejected in Standing Orders in 1846.

> 'I have received the notice to take part of the Misses Gotobed's field for the Railway and I shall be happy to render Mr. Cuming every assistance in forwarding the interests of the ladies.

> 'Mr. Cuming has appointed to come to me on 25th; he has been much engaged on some other lines. Mr. Swaffield has been employed by several parties on the Line and as he was raw at the Trade he came to me for advice, which I was glad to give him, and amongst other things I read over to him Mr. Wing's letter on the subject. This gave him greater confidence to engage with an experienced hand like Mr. Sanders. In return for the hints he had from me, he has given me the result of his dealings and I find that Mr. Sanders has for the Company acted liberally, and I think takes very sound and proper views, though in some cases when imposition is intended (Colonel Leclercq to wit), he has been very firm and decided and has directed the Company's Agents to hand over the amount claimed to the Accountant General in order to have the sum assessed by a jury.

B

'I apprehend as soon as Mr. Cuming has been here, there will be no difficulty as to the farming land, but in the conversation I have had with Mr. Sanders he appeared thereon struck at the prices I told him were made of building ground at Bedford, and I requested him to ask Mr. Pearse what *his* experience was in such matters.

'The station will still be at St. Leonards. In giving the Notice, Mr. Pearse informed me that the application for the site of the station would remain unmade at present, because until they know whether they get the "Extension to Cambridge" Act they do not know how much station room they require. They therefore at present stop the main line abruptly at St. Leonards, and the line crossing the New Road and going through Misses Gotobed's field is the branch to the River only and is not to be *the* terminus – or what may probably be the Central Station for the "Second Derby".

'With respect to the price to be asked for Misses Gotobed's and the Duke's adjoining Land all of which I consider most desirable for building and for sites for business, I think we may expect to get after the rate of Twelve Hundred pounds an Acre, and my reason is that for the St. Paul's Land we obtained that Sum, and we know that many Lots were resold at an advance of 50 per cent, and some of the low priced back ground is, I believe, worth nearly double what it sold for. Then the late Mr. Palmer's field averaged about 6d. per foot which is £1089 per Acre. There was only one frontage and a great depth. It is true that 2 Lots only fetched 3¾d. per foot, but that was because it was well known Mr. Tacy Wing wished to have it and purchasers did not bid against him. The adjoining lots sold for 6½d. and 8d. per foot. Now Misses Gotobed's field has two frontages, and if we take two frontages each 100 feet deep at shilling per foot and the back ground at sixpence or even fourpence it will come to about the price I say.'

By February 1846 negotiations were well advanced and the purchase price of the ground had been agreed. Thomas Bennett negotiated the sale on behalf of the Duke, and eventually agreed on £1,000 an acre. The Duke of Bedford received £4,756 11s, and his tenants £243 9s, making £5,000 in all.

The construction of the railway proceeded during the winter of 1845 and the spring and summer of 1846. This work could not develop without money and calls on the shareholders were made from time to time, as shown by this notice in the *Bedfordshire Times* for 27th December 1845:

'Bedford and London & Birmingham Railway
2nd call of £5 per share

Notice is hereby given that the Directors have this day made a second call of £5 per share on every share in this undertaking and have ordered and appointed that the same be paid on or before 24th day of January next to Thomas Barnard Esq., Banker at his bank, St. Paul's, Bedford, or to Messrs. Glyn Hallifax Mills & Co., bankers, at their banking house, Lombard Street, London.

Interest at the rate of £5% per annum will be charged upon the amount of calls remaining unpaid from the said 24th day of January next, to the time of actual payment.

Dated this 23rd day of December 1845
by Order of the Directors
Theed Pearse Jnr. Secretary'

The terrain between Bedford and Lidlington is flat, but between Lidlington and Ridgmont stations the line had to climb Brogborough hill, and this involved a gradient of 1 in 105 – a serious encounter for the weak engines of the period. Thereafter the gradients are easy, but an added obstacle to railway operating was, and is, the number of level crossing gates to be worked, fifteen in sixteen miles. The architecture of the station masters' houses and the cottages for the crossing keepers was of a pleasing half-timbered design. A less satisfactory feature was the saving of money by building very low platforms which, at Millbrook, Lidlington and Ridgmont are still something of a hazard for older people.

By October 1846 the line was ready for inspection, but heavy rains caused earthworks to slip so that the opening day was postponed until 17th November 1846. The Victorians celebrated the opening of their railways with gusto, and these are described in chapter 8.

The new route to London from Bedford attracted the custom it deserved. It was 2½ hours by train, 3rd class 5s 3d, compared with 4½ hours by coach, fare £1 1s.

Catherine Young, whose experiences of coach travel are given in chapter 1, was now the wife of the Reverend George Maclear, the Chaplain to Bedford Prison. Her diary tells us a good deal about ordinary life in Bedford, and we see the difference the railway made.

'Tuesday 17th November 1846 – the railroad opened
Thursday 19th November – Walked to the station
Friday 18th December – George went to Bletchley to meet Isabel and brought her home.'

By 1848 the stations in Bradshaw were Bedford, Marston, Lidlington, Ridgmont, Woburn Sands, Fenny Stratford and Bletchley. No additional stations were built, but in 1905 there was a burst of activity among railway companies along their branch lines in an effort to combat the new menace of road competition. The idea was to open halts and to have 'motor trains' serving all stations and halts frequently. These were opened as follows: Kempston & Elstow; Kempston Hardwick; Wootton Broadmead; Wootton Pillinge; Husborne Crawley; Aspley Guise; Bow Brickhill. As these halts were at ground level, special coaches were built fitted with steps which swivelled round at the halts to allow passengers to mount. With the steps in this position the brake was fully applied and could not be released until the steps had folded back close to the side of the coach.

During the 1939–45 war the Kempston & Elstow, Wootton Broadmead and Husborne Crawley halts were closed and never re-opened. Wootton Pillinge was renamed Stewartby in 1935.

Two years after the inauguration of the Bedford Railway the county witnessed another opening. The London & North Western Railway (successors to the London & Birmingham in 1846) were naturally anxious to develop their system as much as possible. They already were connected with Aylesbury (1839), Northampton (1845) and Bedford (1846); they had also proposed a branch from Wolverton to Newport Pagnell (1845) although this was postponed for twenty-two years. The Dunstable railway running from Leighton Buzzard to Dunstable would enable them to tap the traffic in south Bedfordshire, and the branch was opened on 1st June 1848.

The Dunstable Railway left Leighton Buzzard in a southerly direction with a sharp curve to the east, all on a fairly steep gradient. This made very hard work for locomotives hauling trains of wagons loaded with chalk from the direction of Stanbridge. However there was worse to come for trains going to Dunstable, as the town lies in the Chilterns, and had to be approached by a formidable gradient of 1 in 40 (in parts) which was also a test of engine efficiency. An intermediate station, called Stanbridgeford, was opened between Leighton and Dunstable and became fully operational in 1860. Although the platforms were of wood and the station was nearly two miles from Stanbridge on one side and Totternhoe on the other it occasionally became very busy. This was when Volunteer Regiments had a field day. Otherwise it was always very quiet.

The line to Dunstable was a pretty and a useful branch. Freight traffic, particularly chalk, was always good, but passenger traffic fluctuated. In the days of 'workmen's tickets' early morning trains were well filled, and towards the end of its days, football matches in Luton on Saturdays would fill the trains. There were seven level crossings on the branch, unimportant in 1848, but the cause of much trouble today. The train services will be found in Appendices A5 and A6.

CHAPTER 3

THE GREAT NORTHERN

The Great Northern was a late-comer, and had to fight for both its construction and survival. The Great Northern Railway Bill was bitterly opposed by the London and North Western Railway, by the Midland and by the Eastern Counties. At the outset there were two companies, and the Direct Northern Railway and the London & York were foes in the early 1840s, but combined in the face of the formidable opposition. When the line was built it served few large cities – the first was Peterborough, 76 miles from the Maiden Lane terminus, and then there were only Lincoln and Retford before York was reached by the grace and favour of other lines. The Great Northern was superbly built, which is hardly surprising as William Cubitt was the engineer and Thomas Brassey the contractor. The company were fortunate in having an able chairman in Edmund Denison, MP, who appointed Cubitt after Joseph Locke had had to resign the appointment, partly because he was busy building lines in France.

While the Direct Northern and the London & York were still in competition, they are mentioned in the Bedford Estate correspondence. The Woburn Steward, Thomas Bennett, wrote to the Agent-in-Chief on 19th April 1844:

'I had only heard that there were two Lines of Rail proposed to York, and a branch among others to Bedford – but I have heard nothing of the merits of the competing lines – the Biggleswade people will undoubtedly make the best fight they can to obtain their line and so will the others; the 17 miles of saving distance is a trifle in favour of the short line, if the longer one should be a much cheaper one to make – as all persons (or at least the great majority) are now aware if a Line of Rail is to go through a Country the more closely it approximates their property or business the better for them. No doubt each line will have its supporters.'

The next letter, written nine days later, hints at the struggles which went on below the surface:

'I saw Mr. Fowler solicitor of Huntingdon yesterday, who appears to be interested in the direct Line of Rail to the North – he had been to Hitchin; Lord Dacre has taken the Biggleswade line favourably Mr. Radcliff holds aloof, but I suppose he will come in; Mr. Hawkins supports it. Mr. Fowler was anxious to see Mr. Tycho Wing as the proposed line will go near to Stibbington . . . '

In 1844 the Direct Northern Railway ordered their engineer, Sir John Rennie, to survey a route which went through Hitchin, Biggleswade, Sandy and St Neots. A year later another survey was made by John Miller who planned to go a mile east of Rennie through Letchworth, then to Biggleswade and Sandy, but a mile west of the 1844 route in order to serve Eaton Socon. Also in 1845 the board of the London & York instructed Samuel Hughes, their engineer, to plot a route and he chose more or less the final Great Northern path except that after Hitchin he wanted to go through Henlow, skirt Biggleswade to the west and come in again at Sandy. In this part of England then, he and Cubitt agreed very well. It was in 1845 that the two companies amalgamated and secured the Great Northern Railway Act of 1846. A letter dated 6th December 1844 from Bennett to Haedy is therefore pertinent:

'Mr. P. [Theed Pearse, the Bedford solicitor] informs me the York and the Direct Northern Lines are about to join, and thinks it is most probable the Girtford branch will come to St. Leonards. He says he has no knowledge of the Bedford and Ely promoters but thinks the professional men are respectable. I asked his opinion of it as a speculation to which he replied it would do the proprietors no good, and ruin the Navigation. He also expressed alarm at some obstruction likely to be formed to the passage of water in flood times by crossing the vale oftener than in his opinion was necessary.

'I suggested if the Navigation and Mill interests could be satisfactorily arranged and to be cleared away, whether his opinion would remain the same. He said certainly not, that he had thought of such a thing but it appeared too visionary. I laughed, and as he is of a speculative turn, I said "nothing in these days was too visionary". I then stated to him my views and opinions as to the great effect to be produced by the complete drainage of the whole vale of the Ouze and the great local and public advantage to be gained by the increased extent to land to be brought into cultivation, causing a great demand for labour and increase of food; the two grand things we must call for with so large a population. He said he had never looked at it in such a light but thought it a subject of very great importance, and one that ought not to drop without further enquiry and examination.'

When in time the Great Northern Railway obtained their Act, they rendered most of the Ely and Bedford line unnecessary, and we hear no more of this company. A letter from Bennett to Haedy dated 3rd January 1845 again shows the Estate's attitude to the various lines:

'The Duke gave me this morning all the Notices for Beds. Railways which have been forwarded to him – also the forms of Assent or Dissent. They are –

One from the Dunstable & London Branch – it touches a small piece of His Grace's land in Totternhoe. It is of little personal interest to His Grace, but as the Dunstable people are anxious for the Rail there is no objection for the Duke giving assent to it.

Four forms from the London & York. The Duke is favourable to the Main Line and has signed, or will sign, a Memorial to the Board of Trade (which Mr. Whitbread is getting up) to this effect, but these forms are in respect of the Branch from Girtford to Bedford, which is objectionable as at present proposed. I am of opinion the Duke should dissent from the Branch Line as now proposed.

Two from the Direct Northern. This branch is better for Bedford than the other. It is probable in this case His Grace will dissent or be neuter, as he cannot be a supporter of both Main Lines to York.

One from the Ely & Bedford. This may be a case in which to remain neuter.'

As the Duke of Bedford was a shareholder in the Bedford Railway (Bletchley to Bedford) which had its terminus at St Leonards, he wanted any other branch line entering Bedford to form an end-on junction at St Leonards. This would greatly increase the importance of the Bedford Railway and give an outlet to the East. The London & York Railway's branch from Sandy would have terminated in St Cuthberts which would have given passengers a long walk through the town. This explains Bennett's letter to Haedy of 12th February 1845.

'I send you a Letter which I received from Mr. Foster of Biggleswade with a copy of plan and sections of the London & York Line and Branch to Bedford . . . I think it is proper they should know any branch to Bedford not terminating in St. Leonards at the London & Birmingham Terminus will meet with the Duke's opposition.'

On 30th August 1845 Bennett wrote again. He returns with greater emphasis to the use of St Leonards station by other branch lines which might enter Bedford, and he refers to Robert Stephenson's plans for a railway linking Bedford with Cambridge. This was surveyed in 1845, and would have run through Tetworth, Waresley and Long Stow, and of course would have been an extension east from St Leonards. It was defeated in Standing Orders, and Bedford had to wait another seventeen years before a line was completed. He refers also to the Northampton Bedford & Cambridge Railway. This was surveyed by Purdon in 1845, and it would have run to St Leonards, and not to St Cuthberts as Bennett feared. The project was abandoned. The Direct London & Manchester, which also belongs to 1845, also came to nothing.

'I met Mr. Fowler of Huntingdon two days ago who is much interested in the London & York line; he professed to be (on behalf of the Company) most anxious to secure the approbation of the Duke of Bedford to their Scheme. I reminded him that Mr. Foster of Biggles-wade had already had communication with us and that he had been informed that the Duke, so far as his Beds. Estates are concerned, was satisfied with their Trunk Line, but not with their Bedford Branch terminating at St. Cuthberts, and that if this was persisted in, they must expect his Grace's decided opposition to the Branch, to which Mr. Foster did not hold out any positive promise that the Terminus should be altered, but only that it *might be* . . .

'Mr. Fowler then said there was an impression that Mr. Foster was treated rather "cavalierly" by us. I said . . . he could judge for him-self, and that neither disrespect nor discourtesy to Mr. Foster or the Company was meant or intended, at the same time I pointed out to Mr. Foster that by their own map . . . it did appear that Mr. Foster and the Biggleswade people only intended us to have an Eastern communication by or through their town and thence to Huntingdon and that however good a "Ruse" it may be for certain Coal Mer-chants to break the Line of communication at Bedford, the interests of the public are not to be sacrificed to petty Local Trade. I also said that now that the Bletchley Act was obtained, our reasons were still stronger for requiring a continued and uninterrupted communication from the West to the East, and that no Line to the East of Bedford which will not run from St. Leonards, or at least afford an easy com-munication with that Line, can be satisfactory to us in the west.

'You will see by the Map that a Line from Bedford to Cambridge is much better than by Huntingdon, for by Cambridge there is direct communication with Lynn, Norwich and Ipswich.

'Mr. Pearse and the Bletchley parties by their shilly shally conduct kept back their plans till the Northampton and Bedford and Cam-bridge Line was announced, and so far as Bedford and Cambridge are concerned we have now two lines projected. I fear if the North-ampton people go on, that we may lose the continuation from St. Leonards as the Northampton will most likely act with the London & York and run into their terminus at St. Cuthberts. It is important to prevent this and an endeavour must be made to reconcile the Jealousies and Jarring Interests of the Solicitors and Engineers. This can only be accomplished by a good understanding with the different landowners interested in the Lines.

'I am of opinion from these circumstances [that] the time is now arrived when the Duke will be compelled to state his opinion and Inclinations, lest we are to be [told] hereafter "that His Grace was too late, and the time is then gone past for attending to his opinions and views".

'I learn from Mr. Sharman that negotiations are in progress for an amalgamation of the London & York, Bedford & Leicester, and Rastrick's London & Manchester. The outline is this: the London & York to make their Line to Hitchin, the Bedford & Leicester to take up from Hitchin, and the Manchester people from Leicester to Manchester, the Yorkists making a branch to Luton from Hertford, and from Shefford to Clophill and Ampthill (if Lord De Grey is so anxious to have a rail near to Silsoe as he is said to be). If this junction should proceed they will form a very strong party and Remington's Independent Line will have little or no chance of success. Provided Oakley is not more infringed upon, I believe the Junction Line is the best to support on account of its being more likely to be effectually carried out. The rest of the projected branches are originated by local Solicitors and supported by the Birmingham, or by the Yorkists, between which parties there appears to be most extreme Jealousy, but it is very foolish for parties between these Two great Lines to permit themselves to be carried away by the partisans of these contending Trunks. The best policy appears to be to avail oneself of, and take advantage of, communications on both sides.

'Interested as the Duke is in the Bletchley both by the Shares he holds and by the property he has adjoining St. Leonards, he must naturally support the Extension, unless the Northampton people have a better Line, and I think His Grace might fairly use his Influence with Mr. W. B. Higgins (who takes up the Northampton Line very warmly) to obtain his support and advise the Northampton Line to run into the Extension, unless as I said, they show a better Line, and then His Grace in that case need not hesitate to advise the Extension to give way to their opponents, securing a junction at St. Leonards.

'Mr. Pym [of Sandy] is said to dislike the Extension as it interferes with his property. I have enquired of Mr. Pearse if he knows whether the line is objectionable to Mr. Pym. Mr. Pearse says that he thinks *not* on personal grounds, but as an anxious promoter of the London & York, Mr. Pym with the Company are opposed to the Extension. If Mr. Pym's opposition is not personal but only as one of the London & York promoters, I should think that may be got over, and for the sake of securing the Extension, and for promoting the general public utility I think the Duke might be recommended to give his Sanction to the London & York; Bedford & Leicester; and Rastrick's Manchester, in preference to Remington's Independent Manchester.'

However, in spite of everything the Great Northern Railway Act was passed on 26th June 1846, and among the directors was F. Pym of Sandy. The branch line to Bedford:

'shall commence by a junction with the said main line in the said parish of Sandy and shall pass through Sandy, Beeston, Girtford, Blunham, Northill, Moggerhanger, Willington, Cople, Cardington, Eastcotts, Goldington, St. Cuthberts Bedford . . . and shall terminate at or near a street called Back Street in the said parish of St. Cuthbert.'

By the time the Bill was passed it had cost the company £432,620, and as Brassey, the contractor, said 'it cost less than this to build the whole of the Turin-Novara Railway in Italy'.

Then began the almost interminable job of negotiating with the landowners on the route for the purchase of the land and buildings. The Railway Company had, of course, compulsory powers, but they were used with discretion, for there was no point in making enemies unnecessarily. Over a distance of 14 miles, from Hitchin to Sandy, there were 126 separate parcels of land. Where the track went right through buildings, it was usual to have them re-erected nearby.

The solicitors acting for the Great Northern Railway in London were Baxter Rose & Norton of Westminster, who had their agents in this county. The first action to be taken by solicitors was to send out a statutory notice of their intention to use certain lands, which were specified on the copy plan and schedule lodged with the Clerk of the Peace at Bedford. Each owner was required within twenty-one days to deliver at the office of Messrs. Baxter Rose & Norton a statement in writing giving the particulars of their estate, and the amount of money they claimed as compensation for the value of the lands, and of any injury and damage.

The owner of the property generally consulted his solicitor, and then used an estate agent to determine the value of the land or buildings, and the injury or damage he was likely to suffer.

S. B. Edwards of Arlesey Bury Farm first got in touch with his solicitor, Mr T. Hine of Bedford, who wrote to Baxter Rose & Norton on 4th March 1847:

'S. B. Edwards, Esq., the landlord intends claiming for the farm house and homestead to the east of the intended line . . . You will therefore oblige me by stating by return of post what are the views of the Directors . . .

'I shall take it for granted that my neglect to claim for the same shall be no barrier to a claim at a future day.'

Mr Swaffield, the Ampthill auctioneer and estate agent, was called in by Mr Edwards, and he obtained an estimate from J. T. Wing, the Bedford architect, for the work to be done:

'Arlesey Bury Farm

I estimate the expense of building the house and homestall on the Bury Farm at Arlsey the property of Samuel Bedford Edwards Esq., providing all new materials and giving the same accommodation as at present afforded to be placed on a different site at £2,174.

For rebuilding Mr. Edwards' private homestall as above at £560.

For removing the Hermitage homestall and building one new cottage at £260.

Jos. Tacy Wing, 6th March 1847'

It is evident that the line is going right through the farm and the Company will have to provide fresh accommodation. However, while negotiations proceeded, Mr Edwards died. His claim was pressed by his Trustees, but disputed by the Company, who had appointed W. T. Nash, a valuer of Royston, to act for them on local matters. We therefore have a second estimate for the same work:

'To William Thomas Nash Esq.

I hereby propose and agree to take down, remove and rebuild the farm house and buildings, fences and gates forming the farm homestall at Arlsey held by Mr. Inskip together with all the inside fittings and including digging and bricking a well 30 feet deep and boring the same 120 feet deep for the sum of £1,350 and also to take down remove and rebuild the Hermitage Barn stable and bullock house for a further sum of £120 the whole to be left in good tenantable state of repair.

Witness my hand this 15th day of May 1847
Luke Gimson, builder, Royston'

A letter from Baxter Rose & Norton, dated 7th July 1847 refers to the difference of opinion, and the appointment of an umpire:

'3 Park Street,
Westminster

W. T. Nash, Esq.   7th July 1847
Dear Sir,

re S. B. Edwards' Trustees

Mr. Hubbard, the acting Trustee of Mr. S. B. Edwards's Estate has been with us as to the difference between your estimation of value and that of Mr. Swaffield and as the Lands Committee are very anxious to avoid having recourse to a Jury if possible they have instructed a London surveyor wholly unconnected with the Company to pro-

ceed to Arlsey to make a special report. We are directed to beg of you
to furnish us by return of post with the detailed particulars of your
valuation with a full statement of your views on the subject, containing such information as it is desirable to place before this gentleman to enable him to arrive at a proper conclusion.

Baxter Rose & Norton'

Nearly eighteen months later agreement had been reached between the
Great Northern Railway Company and the Trustees not only on the
Arlesey Bury Farm, but also on all the other parcels of land which were
being disturbed by the construction of the railway.

'The purchase money for the said land and hereditaments is to be
£3,280.

'The sum for the removal and rebuilding of the buildings standing
upon the land numbered 72 is to be £450.

'The sum for slating and tiling of the Hermitage House and buildings (now only thatched and will be endangered by fire from the
near vicinity of the said railway) and for putting up 6 feet high fence
between several premises to be £250, and lastly for residential injury
– £1,320 making altogether £7,000, Which it is hereby also agreed
shall include compensation for damage to be done to the remaining
estate which could have been awarded by a Jury under the provisions
of the several Acts of Parliament made in this behalf.'

The company agreed to make and maintain several crossings.

Legal and valuation work increased considerably with the coming of a
railway, and many professional people wished to share in this temporary
prosperity. W. T. Nash, the Royston valuer who has been mentioned
above, originally wrote to the Board of the Great Northern Railway and
was told to call on Baxter Rose & Norton, but on 1st March 1847, after
his visit, they wrote to him:

'Immediately after . . . seeing you . . . we received directions from
the Board to forward all the notices and other information relating to
the district between Sandy and Hitchin to Mr. Woolley of Colling-
ham Manor, Newark.'

Nash wrote again to the solicitors, only to be told on 4th March:

'We duly received your favor of the 3rd but the subject is one
entirely for the consideration of the Board.'

Not easily put off, Nash wrote direct to the Secretary of the Great
Northern Railway, who replied on 6th March:

'I have to acknowledge receipt of your letter of 5th with an enclosure, being copies of correspondence relative to your employment

as a Land Valuer on behalf of this Company, and the same shall be laid before the Directors at the first opportunity as you request

I. R. Mowatt, Secretary'

Nash's initiative was successful, and on 1st April 1847 his appointment as valuer was confirmed.

If the acquisition of privately owned land brought complications, the purchase of common land brought them tenfold. It became usual for a committee to be formed by those having an interest in the common land; thus the Arlesey Common Committee wrote to W. T. Nash on 9th July 1847 asking him to treat direct with the Committee in the future. There was also a large common at Biggleswade and the Committee appointed wrote to Nash on 12th July as follows:

'*Great Northern Railway and Biggleswade Commoners*
The following persons having been duly appointed a Committee to treat with the Company herein pursuant to the Lands Clauses Act, we shall thank you to treat with them so that a contract may be forthwith entered into:

'William Hogg. Robert Lindsell. John Nathaniel Foster. William Pope. Charles Nash.'

One of Nash's correspondents was John Ransom, a miller, and a member of the Society of Friends.

'15th April 1847

John Ransom takes the liberty of informing T. W. Nash that he has deputed S. Swaffield of Ampthill Park to settle his claims on the Great Northern Railway. S. S. will expect to hear from T. W. N. when he is to attend to the business.'

'29th July 1847

Respected Friend,
We have signed the agreement as thou wilt see after inserting a provision against any support of the bridge being placed in the mill stream. The copy having thy signature should have the same words inserted and is for that purpose returned.'

The cost of purchasing the land was heavy. In 1847 Rowley Son & Royce of Royston dealt with sixty-seven owners of land and property and settled their claims for £34,000; Samuel Swaffield of Ampthill handled the claims of thirteen owners between Little Barford and Ippolitts and settled for £23,772.

Apart from purchasing the site of the line itself, the company could, and did, serve notices on owners of adjoining land when it was necessary to make a temporary road from the highway to the railway. Heavy and bulky construction materials might be wanted and the easiest way to get them to the contractor could well be to make a road direct to where he was then working. This notice, served in 1849, helps us to realize the disturbance to ordinary life that the coming of a line could cause.

'The Great Northern Railway Company do hereby give you notice, that under the powers of an Act of Parliament passed in the session held in the 9th and 10th years of Her present Majesty intituled "An Act for making a railway from London to York . . ." the said Company intend at the expiration of ten days from the service of this notice . . . to enter upon the lands described, referred to in the plan annexed, and coloured yellow, for the purpose of forming roads thereon to or from, or by the side, of the said railway.

'The said Company hereby further give you notice, that the Company are bound, within one month after their entry on the same lands . . . to pay to the occupier thereof the value of any crop or dressing that may be thereon, as well as compensation for any other damage of a temporary nature which such occupier may sustain . . . and also to pay half-yearly during their occupation . . . a rent to be fixed by two Justices in case of dispute and also within six months after they have ceased to occupy the said lands to pay to the owner and occupier . . . compensation for all permanent or other loss damage or injury which may have been sustained . . .

J. R. Mowatt
Secretary to the G.N.R.
22nd October 1849

To William Edwards owner
Joseph Cooper occupier
0 Acres 0 Rods 11 Perches in the parish of Biggleswade.'

Although the first trains on the Great Northern ran in 1850, alterations to the alignment were constant as, for example, when it was found that traffic necessitated the construction of more sidings. Some widening of the lines was made in Biggleswade in 1851 and on this occasion the claim was not for damage to property but loss of profit. It appears that Stratton Street, Biggleswade, was blocked in January 1851, and the thirsty inhabitants of the town who had been in the custom of visiting a public house kept by one George Chessum had gone elsewhere. The brewers, Cristy & Sale of Ashwell, Herts, soon took the matter up with the Company, and the Great Northern agreed to pay £1 16s a week for as long as the street was obstructed, representing the loss of profit on the sale of beer.

It was not only the area of land taken, but the loss of cultivation due to severance (i.e. the residue of the fields might be too small for satis-factory cultivation) that called for compensation. However, when Rayns-ford's Trustees claimed £277 10s for 1a 2r 3p of land taken and severed at Arlesey in 1857, no one can suppose that any owner undervalued his loss.

The first Great Northern train left the Maiden Lane terminus in London on 8th August 1850. It was a 'Parliamentary' and covered the 76 miles to Peterborough in 2½ hours. This was a modest start, but it was the begin-ning of what was to become one of the best lines in the kingdom. The Great Northern, never a rich company, had to postpone the last mile or so into King's Cross until 1852. There were expensive tunnels to bore, and the building of a terminus worthy of such an undertaking. The opening day for the terminus was 14th October 1852. King's Cross is a splendid example of 19th century functional design, surviving bomb damage during the last war, and today still serving the purpose for which it was built.

Cubitt built the line well. With less money per mile at his disposal than Robert Stephenson had had for the London & Birmingham, he had to be content with gradients of 1 in 200 (Stephenson insisted on 1 in 333). But he was helped by going through the flatter part of the countryside. Coming from London, it was hard work for the engines until Potters Bar was passed, then came an easy run down to Hatfield. Over the river Mim-ram and the valley at Digswell went the lovely viaduct which today carries locomotives weighing well over 100 tons just as well as it did the small Sturrock engines of the 1850s. There was a 'hump' at Woolmer Green, but some fast running was possible through Bedfordshire, with another hump at St Neots.

Each railway had its own style of architecture and it is impossible not to recognise the Great Northern touch not only in the more obvious station buildings but in the small lineside workmen's cottages. Another typical Great Northern feature was the 'somersault' signal so called because its arm swivelled about a centre pivot. This was adopted at great expense after the accident at Abbots Ripton in 1876 which was caused by signals working in slotted posts being clogged by snow and remaining in the 'clear' position instead of returning to 'danger'. The apple green livery for passenger engines and the varnished teak coaches made an admirable turn out.

The southern part of the main line was commendably free from level crossings although those at Arlesey station, Everton crossing and Temps-ford station have persisted. Arlesey is now (1969) being replaced by a bridge. Arlesey, Biggleswade and Sandy were original stations, with Arlesey Siding (later Three Counties) opened in 1866 and Tempsford in 1862. Train services are given in Appendices C1, C2, C3 and C4.

CHAPTER 4

THE MIDLAND COMES SOUTH

The year 1851 found Bedfordshire served by four railways of which three were within the county boundaries. The fourth, the London & North Western, came close to the south-west of the shire and by means of its two branches was serving an area bounded by Woburn, Bedford, Dunstable and Leighton Buzzard. The only main line within the county was the Great Northern, but this did not serve the county town, and Bedfordians wished to have a main line of railway running through their town. Bedford will always be regarded as a Midland Railway preserve and it would be profitable to examine the background and then the rise of the Midland.

The Midland Railway Company began as four small provincial railways which, after joining forces, decided to reach for London. The Midland Counties Railway, the Birmingham & Derby Junction Railway and the North Midland had all met at Derby. Amalgamation was the wisest policy, and the Midland Railway emerged in 1844. The tiny fourth constituent was the old Leicester & Swannington Railway which had started its life in 1832. It owed its beginning to John Ellis and George Stephenson, and its sixteen miles were devoted to the carriage of coal. The Leicester & Swannington had the wyvern of Mercia as its badge, and this the Midland adopted.

Already, in 1845 the Midland was thinking of further expansion. Leicester-Bedford-Hitchin suggested a good geographical route, and at Hitchin either the Direct Northern or the London & York would provide access to London. F. S. Williams in his *Midland Railway; its Rise and Progress*, states that the Leicester to Hitchin route was decided upon because of pressure put on the Midland Board by landowners at Market Harborough, Kettering and Bedford. Then there was the tempting iron ore traffic near Wellingborough, and south of Bedford, William Henry Whitbread was anxious to have the railway through his estate, offering the Midland land at no more than £70 an acre. However, other promoters had the same plans in mind.

During the period known as the Railway Mania three companies sent their surveyors over the Leicester to Hitchin route, while two others did the northern and southern halves respectively. In 1845, the Leicester &

Bedford Railway, with a capital of £1,500,000 plotted a line which, in Bedfordshire, would have gone through Sharnbrook, Milton Ernest, then slightly to the east of the present Midland Road station in Bedford to Medbury Farm near Elstow, and, tunnelling under Hammer Hill, would have reached Hitchin via Rowney Warren. This company's bill was rejected in the Lords; its assets were purchased by the Midland.

George Hudson's name was connected with another attempt to build a line, also in 1845. This was known as the South Midland Railway and was surveyed by Robert Stephenson. The line would have passed close to Bletsoe and Milton Ernest and then would have run into St John's station in Bedford. The bill was mangled in Parliament, and only a small branch from Irchester to Huntingdon received sanction. Again the Midland stepped in and purchased the assets.

The Midland Railway, under John Ellis, was growing fast. In 1846 the company planned its own extension to Hitchin. Hudson was the prime mover, who chose Robert Stephenson as engineer, and the latter had Liddell as his assistant. The route is an interesting one. From Cotton End the line tunnelled under Exeter Wood, past Old Rowney and New Rowney, to the east of Shefford, south of Clifton and exactly where the *Bird in Hand* public house stands today, and on to Hitchin. The capital was £2,250,000 and the bill became law. But Hudson had also wished to see the Eastern Counties Railway, of which he was Chairman, extend from Hertford to Hitchin, and when this bill was thrown out on Standing Orders, the Midland Railway Extension Act lost its value. In 1847, when the act was passed, money was becoming more difficult to raise, and so the Midland drew back, and in 1850 their powers to extend expired.

The London & Nottingham Railway plotted a line through Bletsoe and Milton Grange to Clapham Road, Bedford, but the company was wound up. Finally the Direct Northern Railway (1845) planned to build a branch from Stevenage to Bedford by way of Shefford, Deadman's Cross and Cotton End. However, the company joined the London & York Railway, and abandoned their branch in favour of the London & York's branch from Sandy to Bedford. When both companies became the Great Northern Railway, the Sandy to Bedford branch was included in their 1846 Act, and held in reserve.

In his letters Thomas Bennett, the Woburn Steward, comments on almost every railway. He refers to an important meeting at Bedford in his letter to Haedy dated 20th September 1846:

'I am glad to find that the Railway Meeting at Bedford on Friday passed off very well and the competing parties "King" Hudson and the Midland on the one part, and the Bedford & Leicester on the other, have probably seen the folly of "war to the knife" . . . The Bedford Terminus at St. Leonard's – it is in the Duke's interest to promote those lines that must come there.'

The Duke disliked any line which would run near his house at Oakley. Bennett wrote on 22nd January 1847:

'The Duke signed his Assent to the Luton & Dunstable Railway, and to the Cambridge & Bedford by Biggleswade, but to the Leicester, Bedford and Hitchin his Grace does not feel disposed to assent, on account of Oakley, although he by no means wishes to oppose the scheme . . . [but] no amount of money can compensate him for what he may consider an intrusion on the privacy of his Residence.'

When it appeared that the Midland Railway would succeed in getting their Bill through, the Duke had second thoughts. On 24th January 1847 Bennett wrote:

'I do not think the Midland Company would wish to make a station at Oakley, but I think when the Duke may be staying there, he will not like to have to go to Bedford . . . It would be always a convenience to have Fish, or parcels left in passing by. If therefore, it is of sufficient consequence, now is the time to mention it . . . get an interview with Hudson – as I dare say we can do nothing in it without the full concurrence of His Majesty.'

And two days later 'His Grace would rather no Rail came into the parish [Oakley] but if it cannot be helped, then we would like all benefit from it'.

In 1852 the outcome of negotiations between the Midland and the Great Northern was an agreement to accommodate Midland traffic at Hitchin. The route was re-surveyed by Charles Liddell and John Crossley, and when once the Act was obtained, Thomas Brassey, the greatest of the railway contractors, began construction in 1855. It is reported that John Ellis put a limit of £19,000 per mile on the cost of construction.

By 1857 the line was ready. Although called the Leicester to Hitchin extension, the line began at Wigston Junction, 3·2 miles south of Leicester. The track between Wigston and Leicester was part of an 1840 extension to Rugby. Brassey had built the 63 miles for £1 million, a low figure, and in keeping the cost down followed the contours laid down by Liddell. The road was a very hard one to work for steam locomotives as there were four summits approached by long inclines, including for southbound trains Sharnbrook summit, after four miles up at 1 in 120. This was so severe that when coal traffic became really heavy the Midland built separate goods lines through a tunnel at Sharnbrook, thus easing the gradients. This was part of the scheme for a new line to Nottingham via Melton Mowbray opened in 1880. After Bedford there was another steep ascent from Cardington to Warden tunnel. This was at a climb of 1 in 120. Warden tunnel itself, 880 yards long, was unpopular with enginemen if the wind was blowing from the north-west. Here, heavy goods trains would be travelling at a walking pace and the wind would blow the smoke into the cab of the engine. 'The only way to breathe', said Bert Rogers, a driver from Bedford shed, 'was to get down onto the lowest step at the side of the engine and let the loco take the train through.' The footplate was resumed when fresh air was reached, on the descent to Southill station. Luckily Warden tunnel was dry. If it had been a wet tunnel the engine wheels would have slipped and then the crew would have had to stay on the footplate.

In other ways the line was expensive. From Bedford to Sharnbrook the Great Ouse was crossed seven times; the piers of Sharnbrook viaduct reached their foundations 25 feet below the clay and there was a long brick arch viaduct at Wellingborough. The passenger service commenced on 8th May 1857 but at first passengers had to change at Hitchin on to G.N.R. trains. A better service was provided from 1st February 1858, when Midland trains were permitted to run over Great Northern metals from Hitchin to King's Cross, thus saving the trouble of changing trains at Hitchin. For this privilege, which did not permit Midland trains to pick up or set down passengers between Hitchin and King's Cross, the Midland paid the G.N.R. £60,000 annually.

When the line was ready for opening, John Ellis received the following letter from the Board of Trade after the usual inspection by their officer.

'4th May 1857

I enclose a copy of the report by Lt. Col. Yolland on the Leicester and Hitchin line, and provided only one engine in steam is allowed on the branch to the London & North Western station at Wellingborough and provided a proper passenger station is erected at Bedford within a limited time, my Lords do not object to the opening of the line for public traffic.

Douglas Galton.
Captain. R.E.'

The station which we now call Midland Road was not ready in time for the opening, and the London & North Western Railway allowed the Midland to use their station – the present St John's. Much happened before the Midland station was completed. In the *Bedfordshire Times* of 12th December 1857 arguments were put forward to decide the location of the station. St Mary's was suggested by some inhabitants and strongly urged by the parishioners. This did not at all suit Bedford's tradesmen as is shown in the minutes of the Midland Railway's Board dated 17th November 1857: 'A memorial received from certain merchants, tradesmen and inhabitants of Bedford praying that the station might be constructed on the north side of the river Ouze'. It was resolved that 'provided the Town of Bedford will assist in improving the approaches, the site of the station should be on the north side of the river'.

The minutes for 6th January 1858 reveal that the Mayor of Bedford had written to say that at a Council meeting on 16th December 1857 it had been agreed 'to widen approaches to the station by 40 feet in Well Street and to appoint a Committee consisting of the Mayor, Aldermen Clifton, Kilpin, and Hurst, Colonel Mellor, Mr Jones, Mr Tansley, Mr Bull, Mr Shelton, Mr Read and Mr Eagles to carry out the widening.'

On 18th February 1858 the Midland Board recorded their pleasure to note the progress made in Bedford, and further progress was reported by the Mayor and Mr Turnley when they called on the Midland Directors. In return for what the Council were doing in Bedford the Mayor asked the Railway Company to ease the gradients on the approach to Kempston Road bridge. The Board agreed. The station was finished at the end of January 1859 and the last Midland train to use the L.N.W. station at St John's did so on 3rd February 1859. On 3rd August 1859 the Midland Board's minutes report that property was purchased in Agar Town (near St Pancras), and so it appears that the Board were even then thinking of their own line to London.

The Midland were fortunate in having as their locomotive engineer Matthew Kirtley, who had risen from the ranks and so had a very practical knowledge of the design of steam engines. It was Kirtley who designed the engines to work the newly opened route from Leicester to Hitchin, and he built his machines so robustly that one of them, No. 158A, is now in Leicester Museum. This locomotive was built in 1866 and therefore had an active life of eighty-two years before it was withdrawn in 1948.

The Midland stations between Leicester and Hitchin conformed to a standard design. The platforms tended to be rather low, presumably for economy, and the station buildings were on the small side, of yellow brick and with lattice-type windows set in a cast iron frame. These could be seen until 1962 at Sharnbrook, Oakley, Cardington, Southill and Henlow. Shefford never had good station buildings. The platforms there were of timber, as was the booking hall, until the latter was demolished and a brick-built booking hall and parcels offices were erected in the station yard. The line was commendably free from level crossings. Train services over the years are given in Appendices B1, B2 and B3.

The extension fulfilled the hopes of its originators and it throve only too well; in fact the Exhibition traffic of 1862 demonstrated clearly that the Midland must have their own line to London. When the Hitchin line was part of the main line all was well, but on the opening of the direct London line in 1868, the Bedford to Hitchin line fell overnight to the status of a branch, even though some Midland expresses continued to run to King's Cross, since St Pancras station was not ready in time to receive the new trains. As a consequence, the original double track from Bedford to Hitchin was singled in 1912, but a reasonable service of steam 'rail motor' trains was operated for fifty years thereafter. These gave way to diesel multiple unit trains in 1960 and also some very odd four wheeled rail buses were put on. But the increasing road traffic and the burden of the 1947 and 1953 Transport Acts impoverished the line. Oakley lost its passenger trains in 1958, Sharnbrook in 1960 and Cardington to Henlow in 1962.

This line had an especial debt to William Henry Whitbread who did more than anyone else to encourage the railways to serve Bedfordshire. Above all, it was he who encouraged the Board of the Midland to come south through this county to Hitchin, and because of his work an obelisk has been erected to his memory. It stands on the Whitbread Estate close to Southill station, and could be seen from the train as it left for Shefford. The inscription reads:

'To William Henry Whitbread Esquire For his Zeal and Energy in promoting Railways through the County of Bedford. 1864. Erected by Public Subscription.'

CHAPTER 5

LUTON DUNSTABLE & WELWYN;
BEDFORD & CAMBRIDGE RAILWAY.

The fact that railway connection came to Dunstable before Luton caused little satisfaction in the latter town particularly as a scheme for a railway had been mooted since 1844. There is a relevant letter from Thomas Bennett, the Woburn Steward, to C. Haedy dated 10th May of that year. The Duke of Bedford owned land in Caddington, and Bennett was concerned about severance, i.e. the line so dividing fields that the pieces of land left are difficult to farm.

'I send you a note I have received from Mr. W. Bennett with a resolution passed at Luton as to making a Railway from that place to Leighton. I think this line is a much more feasible one and more likely to pay than that proposed from Bedford to Bletchley, and of much more use to the County and the neighbourhood – for there now exists a very considerable traffic of coals and other goods from the Grand Junction Canal at Leighton to Luton: Luton is also the great straw plait manufactory and the carriage of plait Boxes to the Rail, now that the Coaches are off, must be very great.

'As far as it concerns the Duke I do not anticipate any objection on his Grace's part. I enclose a Tracing of the plot of land in Caddington – you will see that it is entirely cut off [from] the Lewsey farm by the Road from Luton to Dunstable. If therefore it should be selected as a Station the whole of the piece would be eagerly purchased at a good price, and as his Grace has no other property in Caddington it cannot be any object to keep it, if it is wanted for any other use. Should this go on, the Duke's Estate there will have all the advantages to be derived from it, without any of the disadvantages of severance or other annoyances which occupiers are subject to, until the Fences and Fields get put in proper form again, and as from the importance of the trade of Luton, they are almost sure to have a branch either to the Birmingham Line or to the Eastern or Northern if that proceeds (indeed it is not improbable they may in time have both) yet independent of any private interest to his Grace, I think for the general benefit of that part of the County, the branch to Leighton should be encouraged as far as meeting the views of the promoters in giving consent to the sale of the ground, if it proceeds, and not offering opposition to it.'

Luton did in fact have its connection with the eastern side of the county twelve years later.

The next day Haedy replied:

'The Duke takes the same view of it as you take, and agrees that it should be encouraged to the extent you mention, viz: by meeting the views of the promoters to the extent of consenting to the sale of the ground and not offering opposition. Beyond that it is not desirable that the Duke should go.'

A survey of the route from near Welwyn to Dunstable was made in 1845 by Samuel Hughes for the London & York Railway but the scheme was dropped by their successors, the Great Northern. However, the isolation of their town was keenly felt by Lutonians and by 1854 another project was put forward under the title of the 'Luton Dunstable & Welwyn Junction Railway'. A Bill was presented to Parliament on 16th July 1855 for a line to run from a junction with the L. &. N.W.R. at Dunstable across the road now called A5 to a second station in Dunstable at Church Street. The route lay through the parish of Caddington, near Skimpot Farm and Bury Farm to Luton. Here a station was planned in Bute Street and the line, after crossing the Hitchin road was planned to go through the parish of Breachwood Green to New Mill End crossing the Hertford-shire boundary near the *Leathern Bottle* public house. Other stations were planned for Harpenden, Wheathampstead, and Ayot.

The gradients were severe in this hilly district, being up at 1 in 94 from Dunstable to Skimpot, and down at 1 in 90 past Bury Farm, Luton. A supplementary Bill was presented in November 1855 to allow the line to take a more northerly course between the stations at Dunstable later known as 'North' and 'Town'. The promoters had the satisfaction of obtaining their Act on 7th July 1856.

In view of the Duke's interest we might expect that Thomas Bennett would mention the proposals in his letters. On 21st August 1854 he wrote to Haedy, the Duke of Bedford's Agent-in-Chief in London:

'I send you a Herts. paper containing some information on this scheme. The proposed Line . . . will touch upon Lewsey. It seems to me a matter of such importance to the District, as to be deserving the notice and support of the Duke of Bedford both in a public and personal sense.

'Luton being the first Town in the County as a place of business, it is needless . . . to say how much greater it may become . . . nor, how much the Line of Country between Luton and Dunstable . . . will improve in value.'

The L.D. & W.J.R. held its first Ordinary General Meeting at Luton on 11th October 1855. The Hon. W. F. Cowper, MP, referred to the opposition offered by the London & North Western and the Great Northern Railways, which had proved unavailing. The capital was authorised at £120,000 with borrowing powers up to £40,000. A contract for the works costing £92,000 had been let to Jackson & Bean who had subscribed one third of the capital. The directors recommended that the work between Luton and Dunstable should commence at once. The board consisted of: the Rt Hon W. F. Cowper, MP, T. Chambers, MP, J. B. Lawes, J. Waller, L. Ames and H. Thomson.

Most of these gentlemen were on the board of the Hertford and Welwyn Railway which would branch from the east of the G.N.R. main line as the L.D. & W.J.R. would to the west. The ceremony of turning the first sod took place in Luton on Thursday 25th October 1855 and the day was proclaimed a general holiday. The section between Luton and Dunstable L.N.W.R. was opened on 3rd May 1858 but after this happy event, the company began to run into financial difficulties.

As many of the leading figures had interests in both the Luton and the Hertford lines it had been decided to amalgamate the Companies which was accomplished by the Hertford & Luton & Dunstable Railway Act of 1859. It might appear that this step was the right one as the line from Luton to Welwyn Junction was opened on 1st September 1860. But alas, when the new company held a meeting at the Great Northern Hotel, London, only eighteen days later, it was disclosed that they were in debt to the contractors for the sum of £21,000. Mr Parker and Mr Whitbread suggested a further meeting on 21st October but the proposal was defeated. The obvious step was taken on 1st May 1861 which was to apply for an Act to vest the line in the Great Northern Railway which duly came to pass.

In building the station in Luton the company had to purchase land from the Marquis of Bute and the following correspondence between Charles Austin, a local solicitor, and John Cumberland, a Luton estate agent, with Thomas Collingdon, the Bute Estate's agent at Cardiff, is of interest:

'Luton, 26th July 1859

On looking over these papers it appears that £1,283 has been paid on account of this purchase: vizt. £350 which for the purpose of ad valorem duty was apportioned on the conveyance of the land to the Dunstable Road, and £933 paid as a deposit to make up one third of the whole purchase money on payment whereof possession of the whole including seven acres was given to the Company. This will leave £3,500 to be apportioned as purchase money for the ad valorem duty on the present deed . . .

'The draft conveyance is forwarded by book post which we shall be glad to have returned for engrossment.

Charles Austin.'

Austin was a solicitor in the Luton firm of Williamson & Austin, later Austin & Carnley.

John Cumberland, a Luton estate agent employed by the Bute Estate, wrote to Collingdon from Luton on 30th July 1859.

'I enclose you Tracings of the Land proposed to be offered for sale on 25th next month, also a copy of the sale Bill which is now being printed.

'I could not till today arrange with the Railway Company about the altered line at the end of Guilford Street; it is now settled, setting back from the road at the extreme point of your ground 30 feet. This is very important and adds considerably to the value of the land there – the alteration near the station is likewise a great advantage, giving now some good plots with frontages to the Upper Bute Street, which are very valuable. You will see by the tracing I propose to give these a right of way at the back from Guilford Street.

'If you approve of the Lots as laid out I will put the plans in the hands of the Lithographer. Mr Hopkins has seen them and quite approves them.

'I have not drawn out the Bill of Sale of your Cottages not knowing whether you will offer those in Park Road in one or more Lots. On hearing from you this bill shall be printed.

John Cumberland.'

On 23rd September 1859 Williamson & Austin sent a cheque to Collingdon:

'We have received a cheque as under,

Balance of purchase money   £2566
½ yrs Interest due Michaelmas   £125 12s 8d

                                    £2691 12s 8d'

New Mill End, the last station in the county (going east) was renamed Luton Hoo in 1892, and Luton had the words 'Bute Street' added in 1950.

The Dunstable stations bore various names. The G.N.R. station was first known as 'Church Street' but this was changed to 'Town' in 1927. At the north end, Dunstable L.N.W.R. became 'Dunstable North' in 1950.

The Luton, Dunstable & Welwyn Junction railway consisting of nearly 17 miles of cross-country line through mainly agricultural districts was particularly vulnerable after the Beeching Report (1962). It had ceased to be Luton's principal connection with London after 1868 when the Midland line opened. The first loss was goods traffic which was diverted to Luton from the smaller stations in 1963. The passenger service was maintained by diesel multiple unit trains until 1965 when these ceased to run. However, goods traffic in still handled at Luton by virtue of a connecting link made between the two stations in 1966.

For train services see Appendix C4.

Three years before the Great Northern ran their first trains to Luton and Dunstable, a very small line was opened in east Bedfordshire. This was the Sandy & Potton Railway, which despite its short length of 4½ miles, and its short life of five years, has a history of unusual interest. This little line owed its origin to Captain William Peel, the third son of Sir Robert Peel. Although the latter spent most of his life in Lancashire, the second and third sons lived in Bedfordshire. William turned to a Naval career, but he was also interested in his estate, which lay between Potton and Sandy. The opening of the Great Northern Railway in 1850, so near his land, aroused his interest. It seemed obvious that a line of his own, connecting with the G.N.R. at Sandy, would benefit his estate and his tenants, and from 1852 he began to purchase land on the west side of his estate as far as Sandy. Thus when he put his plan into operation it was not necessary to obtain Parliamentary powers, as the railway would be entirely on his own land. Construction of the 4½ miles began in 1855. It curved away from the south of Sandy station and ran east as far as Deepdale, where it curved sharply to the north and climbed up to Potton at a gradient of 1 in 100. It crossed over the Sutton-Sandy road on a bridge of three brick arches.

In 1854 the Crimean war broke out and it was not long before Captain Peel was ordered to the Black Sea. His courage in action, particularly in throwing into the sea a Russian shell which had landed on his ship, earned him the newly founded decoration of the Victoria Cross. At the conclusion of the war he was given the command of the frigate *Shannon* and ordered to China. In the meantime, in England, the construction of the Sandy & Potton Railway had progressed and was ready for opening in November 1857. The Board of Trade inspector having reported favourably, the railway was opened for passengers on 9th November 1857. Captain Peel's mother, Lady Peel, performed the opening ceremony and named the locomotive 'Shannon', after the frigate. There were the usual festivities. However, Captain Peel's end was a sad one. On the way to China, he received orders to go to India where the mutiny had broken out. He distinguished himself at the raising of the siege of Lucknow and when the mutiny was quelled he looked forward to returning to England. But an epidemic of small-pox broke out in India and Captain Peel died on 22nd April 1858, and never saw his railway.

The 'Shannon' was built by the firm of George England in their Surrey works and cost £800. It hauled two coaches and there was also one wagon for goods and one brake van for the guard. Later a rather smaller engine was ordered from the same firm and named 'Little England'. The train services, which were quoted in *Bradshaw* until December 1861 are shown in Appendix C5. As will be related in the second half of this chapter, the Sandy & Potton Railway was merged into the Bedford & Cambridge Railway in 1862, and between 1860 and 1862 'Shannon' was used in the construction of the new line. After 1862 the engine was sent to the London & North Western Railway Works at Crewe for shunting purposes. The next move was to the Cromford & High Peak Railway, a line of formidable gradients. Later in its life the locomotive made its final move to the Wantage Tramway which ran from Wantage Road station (on the Great Western Railway's Bristol main line) to the town of Wantage, the track being laid at the side of the road. Many of us who travelled in that part of the world in the 1920s will either have seen it at work, or else, better still, have travelled in the little train. The 'Shannon' with other engines hauled passenger and goods trains until 1925, when the passenger service ceased. Goods traffic lasted through the 1930s and during the war, but the railway disappeared after 1947. Fortunately the 'Shannon' was considered by the Great Western Railway as being worthy of preservation, and it was beautifully restored in Swindon Works. Thereafter it rested on a plinth and under a tin roof on the down platform at Wantage Road station, and there it remained until the station was closed by the Western Region of British Rail in 1965. It has now been presented to the Great Western Society at Didcot, where it can be seen in steam. More fitting would be to send 'Shannon' back to Potton where its original engine shed still stands in excellent condition on Mr Marshall's farm. Although there were only the two stations on the Sandy & Potton Railway, the driver would obligingly stop almost anywhere if an intending passenger gave the appropriate signal, such as a flag, if his house was adjacent to the railway.

Although Bedford was not in direct rail communication with Cambridge before 1862, the first of several schemes for this dates from as early as 1845. Three surveys were made in 1845 and 1846. The fourth attempt was successful and the route finally adopted was the work of L. A. Gordon in 1858.

There is some very interesting correspondence from Dr Jacob Brooke Mountain, Rector of Blunham. The letters are undated, but were prob- ably written in the winter of 1858–59, and they show that Dr Mountain was not attracted to the railway, but he was prepared to tolerate it pro- vided his financial interests were protected. The correspondence is with Mr Wilkinson, his solicitor at St Neots.

'Blunham Rectory,
Saturday.

My Dear Sir,

I am informed that the projected railway through Moggerhanger is likely to take place and that it will intersect diagonally the arable fields charged with the corn rent so that the landlords will alter the present boundary fences in order to make the fields available for the plough. If so, it is quite clear that the claims of the Rector will be compromised by the operation, and unless due provision for those claims is made in the Act *at the expense of the Company* I shall feel it my duty to join in petitioning against it.

Will you be so good as to communicate with Mr. Turnley on the subject.

Yours always truly,
Jacob H. Brooke Mountain.'

Mr Thomas Wesley Turnley of Bedford was a solicitor for the Bedford and Cambridge Railway.

Another landowner was Edward Henry Dawkins of Moggerhanger House, and he wrote in December 1858 to Dr Mountain:

'I thank you for sending me Mr. Wilkinson's note which I return. I had a hasty view of the proposed line of the railway as deposited with the Clerk of the Blunham Parish. It appears to intersect 21 pieces of land belonging to me – at least my name appeared in the Schedule 21 times. I think it would be very advisable to show our *teeth*. I would readily bite if I knew on whom to fasten.'

The Rector wrote again to his solicitor:

'Blunham Rectory,
Wednesday.

I send you my map on which the proposed line of railway is slightly traced in pencil. Deviations are reserved on each side and the line branches in a "Y" to north and south leaving nearly a mile between the two junctions with the G.N.R. My name does not appear at all in the schedule, though all the other owners, occupiers and parties interested are fully enumerated.

The omission may have arisen from my telling Mr. Turnley's clerks that I have no lands in Moggerhanger Parish. I shall not be a consenting party to the railway, but I shall offer no opposition provided that they give me an equivalent security for my corn rent, and clear me from all legal and other expenses.'

Another letter helps to explain why the Rector had been omitted from the schedule.

'Blunham Rectory,
Thursday.

Mr. Dawkins tells me that the projected railway from Bedford to Cambridge runs through all the lots liable to me for the corn rent. I have had no notice, though the surveyor, Mr. Cheffins, has called to inspect the hay, and two gentlemen from Mr. Turnley's office of Bedford also called with their own map to ascertain the owners of the land; but they said nothing about the corn rent and I did not think of it.'

And lastly:

'Blunham Rectory,
Tuesday.

I am quite willing to be guided by your advice in re Railway. It is personally of no importance to me and I am only desirous to do my duty to the Living. But the unpunctual payment of the Corn Rent is an annoyance.'

Liddell A. Gordon, the engineer of the Bedford & Cambridge Railway, saw his line opened on 4th July 1862, and the first passenger train on 7th. Three days before the formal opening this notice appeared in the *Bedfordshire Times*:

'BEDFORD & CAMBRIDGE RAILWAY

The Directors are desirous of negotiating Loans upon Debenture Bonds under the powers of their Act at the rate of $4\frac{1}{2}\%$ interest per annum, payable half-yearly, on 1st January and 1st July. The Railway will be worked under a Parliamentary Agreement and the interest upon the bond debt guaranteed by the London & North Western Railway Company.

Euston 29th May 1862.   W. Lang. Secretary.'

The railway ran east from St John's station (then known as Bedford L.N.W.) and crossed the Great Ouse and a tributary, with four bridges in a short distance. The Ivel was crossed after Blunham. It is doubtless the number of river bridges which decided the company to have a single line only from Bedford to Sandy, although the piers were wide enough to carry a double track. In the 1939 war although so many lines were duplicated or otherwise widened, it is strange that this stretch of eight miles was left alone, and when, in 1959, the bridges over the Eastern Region main line at Sandy were renewed at a cost of £150,000, no attempt was made to provide a second set of rails. Originally the first station to be met after leaving Bedford was Blunham, as Willington was not opened for passenger traffic until 1903. So far the line was reasonably level, but after Blunham it dipped sharply to the valley of the Ivel, and just where the railway burrowed under the Great North Road, a halt named Girtford was opened in 1938. Unfortunately the 1939 war caused a shortage of staff and the halt was closed to passengers after only two years. It would have been much easier for the railway to cross the Great Northern on the level, but the latter strongly objected and carried the day.

After crossing the Great Northern, the Bedford & Cambridge line curved south into Sandy station, so that you had the peculiar position (also occurring at Trent on the Midland) where trains going to London left the station in opposite directions. The up G.N.R. train to London went south, and the L.N.W. train with passengers for London travelled north. Hereafter the line took over the alignment of the Sandy & Potton railway, curving first sharply to the east, and then to the north with the added burden of a gradient of 1 in 100 up. Just before entering Potton the traveller could see, on the right, the old engine shed which housed 'Shannon'. All the stations so far had been reasonably near the towns and villages they served, but because of the opposition of the Turnpike Trustees at Gamlingay, this station had to be located about 1½ miles from the town. Before the train reached the next station, Old North Road, it had to climb a long 'bank' up to Hayley Woods at 1 in 105 with a similar descent to Old North Road. When the line was opened, the Old North Road was more important than the Great North Road, but in the 1870s, the very narrow bridge at Tempsford was widened, and traffic began to use the Great North. The line now crosses flat but swampy ground lying between the river Granta and the Bourn brook. There was a further station, called Lord's Bridge, before Cambridge was reached.

Although Willington station was almost wholly of timber and Blunham was partly of timber, the stations at Sandy and at Potton were fine brick structures, and the brackets supporting the roof in each case, had the letters 'B – C' cast in them to denote 'Bedford & Cambridge'.

The platforms were of normal height, and no public road was crossed on the level – a well built railway. L. & N.W. locomotives and stock were used, the former being often Allan 'Crewe' type of small dimensions. Other famous types were 'Prince of Wales' and Midland Compounds, but steam gave place to diesel power in 1960.

In its prime, the railway carried plenty of traffic; it was a useful cross-country link and before the coming of the motor lorry, an enormous vegetable traffic was conducted. Fred Chapman of Potton was goods clerk at Potton sixty-five years ago and remembered working late night after night in the summer when the carts from the various market gardeners waited in the station yard to unload their vegetables to catch the night train to Covent Garden market. The London Midland & Scottish Railway was one of the pioneers in diesel traction and a multiple-unit diesel train was run as an experiment for some months on the Oxford and Cambridge lines in 1936. During the 1939 war the branch carried very heavy traffic; passenger trains were normally of four coaches from early L.N.W. corridor stock, the locomotives being Stanier Class 5 engines or his 26xx tank engines. Freight was dealt with by the G Class eight coupled, and these, after the war, even hauled passenger trains during busy summer traffic. In 1940 the Ministry of Transport put in a spur to enable trains to run from and to the Great Northern main line. A special signal box, Sandy West, was erected and lasted until 1960. The underground petrol storage tanks adjacent to the Sandy-Potton road had special sidings built for tank wagons with another special signal box – Sandy Heath.

Regarding signal boxes on the line, the first box was where Bedford St John's No. 1 stands. Later there was No. 2, just opposite the present day bus garage, and there was one called Goldington, situated near the power station, controlling a passing loop. A few years before the war, Goldington box was closed and the loop removed; in the year 1940, No. 2 box was moved from the east end of the station to its present position by the river at Newnham. When the branch was not mentioned in the Beeching plan those of us who used it deceived ourselves that it would be immune as one of the last east-west links. There was dismay when British Rail announced their intention to close, and a great fight was put up by the various local authorities. But the 1962 Transport Act permitted an appeal only in the case of hardship – the meaning of which was to be interpreted by the relevant Transport Users' Consultative Committee and the Minister of Transport. The loss of £97,000 a year could not be challenged. There were many of us on the last train which ran on 30th December 1967. For timetables, see Appendix A4.

CHAPTER 6

THE MIDLAND REACHES LONDON;
BEDFORD & NORTHAMPTON

When, in 1858, the Midland trains began to run over the Great Northern
metals from Hitchin to King's Cross, the Midland management regarded
their trains as providing a main line service. Unfortunately there were
only two tracks in this section of over 31 miles, and the Great Northern
were beginning to fill these tracks with their own trains. The Midland,
despite the sum of £60,000 a year which they paid the Great Northern,
were coming to be regarded as a nuisance. In 1860 James Allport (later Sir
James) had returned to the Midland as general manager, and he was not
one to allow his company to exist as a second best. The junction at
Hitchin was under the control of a Great Northern signalman, and his
instructions, to say nothing of his loyalty, caused him to give preference
to the trains of his own company. In 1862, the year of the second Great
Exhibition in London, the delays assumed gigantic proportions, and 3,400
Midland trains were delayed between Hitchin and King's Cross. Of this
total, 2,400 were freight trains, many carrying coal, and when on 30th
June the Great Northern refused to allow Midland coal trains to stand in
their sidings at King's Cross, it was inevitable that the Midland would
decide to build their own line to London. They already had their own
coal depot at Agar Town near St Pancras.

When the Great Northern saw that they were likely to lose £60,000
a year, they at once offered to quadruple their line between Hitchin and
London. Allport countered by asking for running powers in perpetuity,
The Great Northern offer was only a palliative in view of their own growing traffic, and Allport was only 'playing trains' while pushing on with
his real objective – the Midland Railway London Extension. Liddell and
Barlow, competent engineers, plotted the route, and the Midland Board
had little difficulty in convincing Parliament that their line was essential.
The Bill became law in 1863. If there was any doubt at all in the mind of
the Board that they were doing the right thing, such doubt was removed
by the Welwyn accident of 9th June 1866. A down Great Northern goods
train came to a halt in Welwyn North tunnel owing to a failure of a
boiler tube in the engine. On the Great Northern, as on other lines,
semaphore signals were normally at 'clear' but were placed at 'danger'

after a train had passed. As traffic was regulated on the notorious 'time interval' system, the signals were lowered again after a stipulated interval, and at Welwyn a Midland goods train following the first duly entered the tunnel under clear signals. It collided with the rear of the Great Northern train, blocking the tunnel, and as if this was not enough, soon after an up Great Northern goods train laden with meat from Scotland destined for Smithfield entered the tunnel and collided with the wreckage. The live coals which spilled from the engines' fireboxes quickly ignited the wooden trucks, and the draught through the tunnel and ventilating shafts roused the flames with frightening force. Only two lives were lost but the material damage was one of the worst in our railway history. It was thirty-six hours before a train could go through the tunnel, and the delay to Great Northern and Midland trains is better imagined than described.

The construction of the London extension was handed over to four contractors, of whom the ageing but still most able Thomas Brassey undertook the northern part, i.e. Bedford to Harpenden.

The original plans show that the line would have formed a junction with the Hitchin branch near Elstow, and would then have run southwesterly towards Chimney Corner to where the existing line now runs. This would have meant that a large number of trains would have had to cross the L. & N.W. Bletchley branch on the level – a most undesirable arrangement. A wiser re-alignment resulted in the railway as we know it. After crossing the Great Ouse, the line had to climb a 1 in 176 to clear the Bletchley branch near Cow Bridge, and it dips at the same incline soon after. Powers had to be obtained to divert Ampthill Road at this point. Near Stewartby the Midland had to demolish Magpie Hall as it was in a direct line; the farm buildings of Magpie Farm were visible thirty years ago, although they have since vanished. To reach Ampthill station you pass through Ampthill tunnel, and the original bore was the eastern one; this can be seen quite clearly from the front of a diesel multiple-unit train as the track points straight to this tunnel before curving to the right to pass through the later bore. Before 1939 the *Swan* public house at Astwood was kept by John Wooding, who when young used to walk over to Ampthill to watch the workmen digging the tunnel. A new road had to be made to reach Ampthill station which, in the early days was much more important than Flitwick. The railway has been climbing, mostly at 1 in 200 to Ampthill, but now it falls to Flitwick.

The engineers' plans show the line passing through Flitwick Wood and there was no Flitwick station until 1870. The next station was called 'Harlington for Toddington', and the road between the two villages had to be diverted. The summit is reached 15·3 miles from Bedford in a cutting at Chalton about 60 feet deep. Williams relates how teeth of an immense

D

crocodile and many ammonites were unearthed when the cutting was being made. The line now falls at 1 in 176 to Leagrave, where powers also had to be obtained for a road diversion, and on past Dallow Farm, and so into Luton. South of Luton the line again rises to Chiltern Green where the Midland obtained powers to divert the existing Great Northern branch to Dunstable seven furlongs to the west. The line then continued through Harpenden and St Albans to St Pancras. The first traffic from Bedford, on 13th July 1868, went on the Moorgate Street line, but the new St Pancras station was ready by 1st October in that year, though nearly five years were to pass before Scott's beautiful hotel was ready to receive travellers, on 5th May 1873. However, in 1872 the passenger bookings at St Pancras numbered 171,000 bringing £97,000 to the Midland Railway.

The Midland was now one of our greatest railways, setting fashions rather than following them. In 1873 third class accommodation was included in all trains, a revolutionary step. In 1874 Pullman coaches were introduced, and in fact the first trial was between London and Bedford. The next year second class was abolished and cushions fitted to all third class coaches to cover the bare boards. Nothing could have advertised the Midland better than the decision to change the livery of the locomotives from green to crimson lake in 1883 so that a Midland train was quite outstanding in its appearance. This change was made under the chief mechanical engineer Samuel Johnson, who would have been an artist if he had not designed engines. His most beautiful creation was the 'single driver' of 1896 which was stabled at Kentish Town and therefore was seen at Bedford nearly every day. No. 118 of this class has survived and can be seen at the Leicester Museum.

In 1890 the west curve was put in at Bedford station enabling express trains to pass with undiminished speed. With a view to establishing four tracks continuously from London, another tunnel was bored in Ampthill west of the first one in 1891, and three years later the four track system extended from St Pancras to Glendon North Junction, this distance of 75 miles being the longest in the country. In 1905 the bridge over Hitchin Road, Luton, was widened to accommodate more tracks. In more recent years the Royal Ordnance Factory was opened at Wilshamstead (1941) and this increased the freight traffic on the line. Timetables are shown in Appendix B4 and B5.

There were three schemes to unite Bedford and Northampton before the successful one of 1872: two in 1845 and one in 1864. Charles Liddell surveyed the route in 1864 which was practically the same as the one finally adopted, though the original plan provided for a separate terminus at Bedford. A paragraph in the *Bedfordshire Mercury* of 13th

November 1866 suggests that this idea was dropped because of the enormous demands made by the owners of property, and that by using the Midland station, the company saved £20,000.

The line was opened on 10th June 1872. The railway left the Midland main line at Oakley Junction, and after crossing over the Bedford to Northampton road by a fine stone bridge consisting of a single great arch, arrived at Turvey station – a pleasant stone building. Unfortunately Turvey itself was about one mile away. The line then ran near Clifton Reynes and crossed the Great Ouse just before Olney station, which was attractively built in stone, and conveniently situated. The trains ran into St John's Street station in Northampton, but this was closed in July 1939. There were no level crossings.

After 1945 there was a decline in traffic and services ceased in 1962. Timetables for the 19th century are given in Appendices B6 and B7. Between 1939 and 1962 the trains from Bedford ran into the L.N.W. Castle station in Northampton. Between 1923 and 1939 the London Midland & Scottish Railway used to run excursion trains from Bedford via Olney and Ravenstone Wood Junction to Towcester in connection with the horse racing there.

CHAPTER 7

SCHEMES THAT FAILED

A glance at the railway map of the United Kingdom for, say, 1910 would show so many routes that a student of railway history could be forgiven for thinking that every proposed line had succeeded. Actually many more lines were planned than those disclosed on a map – for example in Bedfordshire nine (including the Sandy & Potton) were constructed and nearly thirty failed. Several of the proposed lines have been mentioned earlier when describing the background history of successful lines, and further details can be found in my typescript account: *Railways of Bedfordshire Planned but not Built* at the Bedfordshire County Record Office.

When a railway was proposed, landowners, business men and financiers would meet and decide to issue a prospectus. This, when circulated, should bring in enough support for a company to be formed, and for engineers to be instructed to plot the route. Competent lawyers had the Bill drafted, and when this was submitted to Westminster, copies of the plans and books of reference would be deposited with the various Clerks of the Peace. In the case of unsuccessful lines, the promoters might get as far as having a Bill presented, or only as far as depositing plans. Others less fortunate would fall by the wayside. One company which did not even get as far as publishing plans was the Boston Bedford and London Railway. This was as early as 1836 and the following letter dated 16th August is from Thomas Bennett, the Steward at Woburn, to W. G. Adam, Agent-in-Chief of the Duke of Bedford at the London Estate Office.

'The Duke gave me a prospectus of the Boston, Bedford and London Railway which had been sent to His Grace, requesting his support, and the Duke desires me to enquire about it. I have, and do not think there is any chance of its being carried into effect, but it has made the Bedford people on the alert, and a Cross Line from Cambridge via St. Neots, Bedford and Newport Pagnell to join the Birmingham, is started, and I think this is likely to answer all the purposes Bedford and the adjoining country may want in that way. This Cross Line is likely to succeed, and I hope it will, as it will give an outlet both East and West. The Bedford people say very truly that if they do not get a Communication with the Main Lines in progress through the Country, they will be excluded from any benefits that are likely to arise from these increased means of traffic.'

In 1844 we begin to hear of the Ely & Bedford Railway. Plans were duly deposited and a Bill presented but in 1846 the rival Great Northern Railway obtained its Act which made nearly all of the Ely & Bedford Railway unnecessary. The following is a letter from Goodwin Partridge and Williams, agents of the Ely & Bedford, to Mr Wilkinson, a St Neots' solicitor.

'Lynn, September 14 1844

We send you a prospectus of the Ely & Bedford Railway and will send a packet as soon as we can obtain them. We have sent a prospectus to all the Provincial committee including the three Gentlemen of your Town. Our advertisements appear for the first time today, but the project has become known in Liverpool through our friend Mr. Lacy, and we have in consequence already received applications from substantial men there for upwards of 2,000 shares.

Will you be kind enough to furnish us with particulars of all public carriages passing through St. Neots mentioning the number of passengers which the coaches are licensed to carry, whether the vans and carriers carry passengers, and the class of goods carried etc. We send a prospectus to each of the gentlemen on the north side of the river upon whom we called the other day.

PS.   We are obliged by your letter respecting water traffic.'

A railway with the imposing title of the Direct London & Manchester Railway received a good deal of attention in newspapers. There is a letter in the *Reformer* (later called the *Hertford & Bedford Reformer*) dated as early as 1st August 1840:

'Sir, In resuming the subject of the London & Manchester Railway let us consider a few of the advantages to be derived therefrom. First to the town of St. Albans. Previous to the opening of the London & Birmingham Railway nearly 100 coaches passed through that town daily and there was also a considerable business doing in posting. Large sums of money were expended in the town and consequently it was in a flourishing state. After the opening of the railway, business vanished. The only inference therefore which we can draw is this – that so soon as the proposed line comes into operation the trade will not only return but increase in a tenfold degree, and what has previously prevented St. Albans from becoming a manufacturing town but the want of a railroad? Independent of this it has many attractions – its ancient Abbey, the monument to Bacon, the celebrated Holy Well, the Town Hall and various other buildings. The air is very salubrious and it is surrounded by the most picturesque scenery.

With such advantages there would doubtless be a great increase in the inhabitants, for when it is brought within an hour's ride of the Metropolis the man of business will eagerly embrace the opportunity to remove to such a delightful spot. He will be enabled to arrive at his office in town in less than an hour from the time he leaves home, and can after the fatigues of the day return to his family in one of the most delightful spots imaginable. House rent will also be cheaper and the expense of a family be considerably diminished.

The town of Redbourn will be benefited to an incalculable extent. This town, it is well-known, received its support solely from the coaches that passed through it, but since the opening of the London & Birmingham Railway everything like business has disappeared: but the time is not far distant when it will not only regain its former station but will be considerably increased. The proposed new line will pass close to it, and during the time works are about business to a great extent must be transacted. It will not however be for that time only, but will secure a permanent advantage. I am sure that every inhabitant on the line will immediately be up and coming and stirring and straining every nerve to promote the cause. The inhabitants of Bedford have already had a meeting; they have taken the matter up in a manner that reflects the highest credit upon them, and I trust that the inhabitants of St. Albans will speedily follow in their wake. If they do not they will have themselves to thank for the loss of the only opportunity of retrieving their fortunes that ever can and will occur.

It is a duty incumbent upon them to do so – the very thing which for the last two or three years they have looked upon as the only means of their salvation is about to take place – which they cannot hesitate for a moment to support.

Yours truly,
Q.E.D.'

On 29th August 1840 the *Hertford & Bedford Reformer* contained the following:

'*London & Manchester Railway through St. Albans, Luton & Bedford*
It will be gratifying to all who are interested in the commercial and general welfare of the line of country from London to the North to learn that all those parties who have taken up arms in favour of this railway are by no means relaxing in their exertions. The London Provisional Committee is formed and a most wholesome regulation has been adopted, namely that two gentlemen from each Local Committee down the line will be privileged to take seats in the

London Provisional Committee as a representative deputation from their own Committee. This will have the effect of uniting the working part of the shareholders – render the proceedings less complicated – and afford greater facility to business.

'The Bedford Borough Committee met on Wednesday; communications from the London secretary were read which put the question as to the line, at rest. It had been the opinion and fear of many parties that the projectors were vacillating between contrary opinions and had not really determined on the line; and that they were coquetting with this, that and the other interest in order to find which was the most weighty. We are glad to find that such suspicions are groundless. The projectors were anxious not to make too strong pledges till the affair was more matured; and therefore they contented themselves with simply ascertaining how far the interest upon the line would go with them in this (we repeat the phrase with all deference to the *Railway Times*) "Great National Undertaking". The projectors through their Secretary Sir Edmond Temple, decidedly affirm that they never contemplated any deviation from the line originally marked out. Great exertions have been made and private interests have been thrown in, *sub rosa*, to entice the projectors to make their line by Biggleswade and thus leave Bedford to shift for itself, and a pretty shift it would be. Indeed another line has been broached but has met with the consideration it deserved. Little spurts of this kind must be expected in all cases where there are conflicting interests, and where an innovation and improvement of any magnitude is contemplated.

'The Bedford County Committee will meet the Bedford Borough Committee at the Shire Hall in Bedford on 4th September.'

However, in due course the London & Manchester was rejected under Standing Orders, and the Board split. Two engineers, Sir John Rennie and G. Remington, launched their 'Direct Independent' railway under part of the Board, while J. U. Rastrick (who had already built the London & Brighton Railway) under the remaining directors continued work on the original route, under the original name. Thomas Bennett of Woburn wrote to C. Haedy on 24th August 1845:

'I will send you the *Northampton Mercury* which contains a Letter against "Remington's Manchester line". I think there is every reason to be satisfied that we are not yet committed to support either – probably better information will soon appear.'

The Duke had been displeased because the proposed Direct London & Manchester line ran close to his house at Oakley, and he had cause for alarm at Remington's revised plan which brought the railway even closer. Bennett wrote to Haedy on 29th July 1845:

'It appears to be proper to reply to the Manchester Line as you propose, for unless they cut through the Hill some way about where the present Turnpike Road passes over it, the property as a Country residence will be completely spoiled; the former plan went almost straight from Bedford to Bletsoe leaving the River to the West of the Line, but by this plan I should say they mean to keep more in the vale to the north of Bedford and cut through Oakley Hill somewhere between Bales farm and Hilton's . . .'

However, Bennett felt more reassured on 13th November 1845 after he had found out that the final course of both the Manchester lines would not, after all, affect the Duke's Oakley property:

'I have just seen the local agents of the amalgamation (Rastrick and Remington) Manchester Line. They have not finally decided on their Line through Oakley, on the west side of Judges Spinney at the deepest cutting through the Hill. The Line will at no place be within sight of the House, and considering that it passes so near it is perhaps as unobjectionable [a] Line as can be obtained.'

However, if the united company could not get a bill through against the bitter opposition of competitors, especially the London & Birmingham, the divided ones were even less likely to do so, and in September 1846 it was announced that both companies had been dissolved.

This was, however, an inventive age. A letter dated 26th October 1845 written by Thomas Bennett to C. Haedy shows that the level-headed Bennett had caught what was called 'atmospheric fever', and he thought that wide turnpike roads would provide ample space for 'atmospheric trains' to run alongside road traffic, to the benefit of the Turnpike Trustees, and of course without alarming the horse traffic, for the trains would be silent.

'I think there is every reason to suppose the Atmospheric principle, which is only yet in its Infancy, may work almost as great a change in the "locomotive department" as that has upon the Turnpike roads.

'I forward you the prospectus of the new London & Birmingham. The projectors reserve for future deliberation the mode of Traction, and I also send you in this a preliminary announcement of a London & Northampton, which you will see is proposed for the Atmospheric, and if this plan can be adopted to the present line of the Turnpike road, it will, I think, meet with supporters along the line of Road and particularly from owners of property in the Towns and villages –

now almost deserted. To the Turnpike Trustees and unfortunate Bondholders the scheme, if successful, will be a god-send, because the present road is generally fifty ft. in width, one Half of which can well be spared and leave plenty of Room for the present Traffic, and as the income from Tolls barely pays interest of Debt and salaries . . ., the parishes through which these Turnpikes pass have the almost certainty of being in a very short time burdened with the maintenance of the Road. Any scheme which will therefore relieve the different trusts from their liabilities will meet with local support.'

Clegg and Samuda were the engineers who patented the atmospheric system of railway traction. Briefly, the invention required the laying of a cast iron pipe between the rails, the pipe being about 18in in diameter. A piston moved along the pipe because stationary steam engines exhausted as much air as possible on one side of the piston, leaving the other side to be acted upon by the normal pressure of the atmosphere. A lug on the piston was attached to the train which often moved very fast. As this projection from the piston had to be partly inside and partly outside the pipe, the latter had a slot running along the top side and this slot was closed by leather flaps, well greased. The wear on the flaps proved to be the Achilles' heel of the system. It was tried several times between 1840 and 1847, but the upkeep was too costly, and the junctions too complicated. However, Bennett was in good company, for Isambard Brunel himself had faith in the system.

The Northampton, Bedford & Cambridge Railway planned in 1845, adopted a route which was in due course copied by the successful 1872 line, and it is the unbuilt line that is referred to by Bennett in the following letter to Haedy, and he mentions, also, another technical problem of railway construction.

'30th October 1845

A line has been last week surveyed from Bedford up the Vale of the Ouze which passes quite in front of Oakley House on the opposite side of the River. I rather suppose it must be the Northampton Line by Turvey. I enquired at Bedford but did not get any information. Our *friend* Ikey (Elger) will probably think it prudent not to be the first to make this communication . . .

We are now having applications for Larch for Railway purposes. Mr. Stephens sold one Lot of ten thousand feet at fourteen pence a foot . . . The contractors decline buying anything but Larch. This is an unfortunate change for the owners of Woodlands. When the London & Birmingham Line was making there was consumption for anything, no matter how rough or coarse, for temporary sleeper, which were taken up and replaced by Stones – now the Stone Sleepers are abandoned and the Larch, after serving the purpose for making the Road, will be relaid . . . in the Road after it is permanently made.'

There were several schools of thought on the correct way of putting down the permanent way (so called because the contractors' rough tracks were 'temporary way'). The most common and the one to be finally adopted was that of laying larch cross sleepers; it was quicker and cheaper to use these than to lay rails on rough wood, and then to have to cart away the rough timber and replace it with larch. Very early railways in the northern colliery areas had used stone blocks three or four feet apart on which to lay the rails. It was found that the blocks were expensive to cut and cumbersome to handle. In addition they had to be tied with cross metal rods, otherwise the road would 'spread'. George Stephenson and Robert Stephenson persisted with the stone blocks after lesser engineers had discarded them, but they began to discard them when working on the London & Birmingham Railway (1838).

A matter which caused a near panic in 1845 was the decision by the Government that all Bills for new railways or extensions of existing ones must be in the hands of the Board of Trade by midnight on 30th November annually, if these Bills were to be discussed in the following session of Parliament. This was because the amount of railway construction with the relevant Bills was swamping normal Parliamentary work. In 1845 30th November fell on a Sunday, and railway officials assumed that Saturday would be the closing day. Many letters arrived at the office of the Clerk of the Peace, Theed Pearse, junior, at the Shire Hall, Bedford, of which the following example is from the solicitors of the Direct London & Manchester Railway, and is dated 11th November 1845:

'As the solicitors for several new lines of railway, we should feel obliged if you could arrange to keep your office (as Clerk of the Peace) open until 12 p.m. on Saturday 29th inst., and if by accident we should be so pressed as to be unable to make the necessary deposits that evening, we should esteem it a very great favour if you would receive our plans and books of reference on Sunday 30th – the last day allowed by the Standing Orders of Parliament.

We shall be most happy to pay you any additional fee you may consider an adequate compensation for this facility being afforded to us.

Crowder & Maynard'

The same request must have been made to the Board of Trade, as the

Board sent a letter to each Clerk of the Peace stating that it was legal to deposit plans on Sunday 30th November 1845.

The south of Bedfordshire would have been served by a proposed Cambridge and Oxford railway which entered the county near Lilley, and passed through Limbury and Lewsey to Dunstable, Totternhoe and Eaton Bray. In the event, only 18 miles between Royston and Hitchin was built, and this eventually became part of the Great Northern. The proposed line crossed land belonging to the Marquis of Bute of Luton Hoo, to whom the two following letters were addressed.

'The Bury, Luton.
11th March 1846.

My Lord,
. . . I embrace this opportunity of mentioning to your Lordship, that the Oxford & Cambridge Railway threatens somewhat to disturb my premises, and that I shall feel obliged if anything can be done (not to hinder the Company, but) to retain my holding inviolate, as there appears to be no *necessity* calling for interference with the buildings and land I hold.

I am my Lord, Your obliged and humble servant,
[the Rev.] Henry Burgess.'

'St. Margarets,
Ware, Herts.
18th April 1846

To the Marquess of Bute.
My Lord,
Having with Messrs. Ray & Collingdon just left the solicitors and agents of the Cambridge & Oxford Railway Company, I beg to forward your Lordship before leaving Town the substance of our meeting subject to your Lordship's approval, and in so doing I am inclined to think your Lordship's objection to the proposed line will undergo some change when it is considered that *none* of the buildings at The Bury will be touched excepting a cart shed on the east side of the said Farm Buildings, and that the sum of about £10,000 will be paid as a compensation for crossing your Lordship's Estate taking altogether about 10 acres of land including the Villas. I hope your Lordship will think favourably of this proposed arrangement which I cannot but recommend provided the Company will accede to it . . .
Wm. Heard'

The Bill was rejected in the Lords except for the little Royston to Hitchin stretch, but while its fate was uncertain, the following letter shows some of the problems it caused to people living along the proposed line. Thomas Hyde wrote on 22nd March 1847 to F. Chase, Steward of the Manor of Luton, which went with the Bute estate:

'I shall be much obliged any time when you write to me, for information concerning the Rail Road, as there are so many conflicting rumours concerning it at Luton, we do not know who or what to believe. There is an Oak Tree, 2 Ash and 4 or 5 Elm standing in 7 Acres close to the proposed line of Rail. Please to say would you like the Elm fell and kept for our own use, and the Ash and the Oak sold, but the Oak if it could be left standing about 3 weeks longer would be more valuable as the Bark would then strip.'

No one could forecast accurately what would happen to a Bill in its course through Parliament. Active support by Members of the Commons could be defeated by interested landowners in the Lords. If an Act passed, there could be financial difficulties, or the line might be abandoned through changed circumstances. Often the outcome kept both shareholders and landowners in suspense.

However, even though a railway might not materialise, the presence of a skilled engineer in the district could be of some local benefit. For example, in 1845 M. Borthwick was surveying the extension of the Bedford Railway to Cambridge (which did not come to pass), but his professional skill was employed in connection with 'The New Cut' which can be seen today at Goldington, and which resulted from collaboration between Thomas Bennett and Captain Polhill of Howbury.

A list of Railway Companies which deposited plans with the Clerk of the Peace in Bedford, but whose projected schemes collapsed from one cause or another, is shown in Appendix D.

CHAPTER 8

RAILWAY OPENINGS

The opening of each of the nine railways in this county has been mentioned, but nothing said about the official ceremonies. The Victorians did
these ceremonies well; the tables sagged with food and the speeches were
verbose. To paraphrase the speeches would be to lose the atmosphere, and
so a few are therefore given as reported in the Bedfordshire newspapers of
the day.

The Bedfordshire Times 21st November 1846:

'*OPENING OF THE BEDFORD & LONDON & NORTH
WESTERN RAILWAY*
EXCURSION TRIP TO BLETCHLEY 17th November 1846
The long-deferred ceremony of opening this railway took place on
Tuesday when the shops were closed, and a general holiday was given
in Bedford. Throughout the morning there were arrivals from different parts of the country; and some thousands of persons made their
way to the station at St. Leonard's, until, at length, every other part of
the town appeared deserted. At 12 o'clock, a large party who had
received the excursion tickets, entered the station, and shortly afterwards the formidable train of upwards 30 carriages, crowded by
nearly 600 passengers, and drawn by two powerful engines, started
amidst strains of music from the Bedford brass band, and shouts
from the assembled multitude – the bells of the parish churches toning
aloud their merry peals. The banks on each side of the line were
crowded with spectators and at every crossing of the roads large
numbers of persons were assembled to witness the passage of the
first train.

'Mr. Randle, the chief agent of the contractor, Thomas Jackson,
Esq., Mr. Storey and the other gentlemen who have been engaged in
the superintendence of the works, were on the engines, pointing out
the gradients on the line, which was necessary in consequence of the
tremendous train, and from the circumstance of the rails being somewhat slippery from the rain which began to fall soon after the train
started. Large parties were assembled at the several stations on the
line, and appeared to take great interest in the event. On arriving at
the famed Brogborough-hill, where the gradient is steep (namely,

1 in 127) the train went slowly, but on reaching the open fields again it went on at a rapid pace, and eventually reached the station at Bletchley about half-past one o'clock. Here the passengers alighted and viewed the extensive works which are in progress, and which are intended to make Bletchley station the most important first-class station on the great line. The engines were turned on one of the new tables invented by Mr. Handcock, which may be termed the perfection of ponderous machinery, and at that moment a train arrived from London bringing Mr. Scott, the engineer, and a party from the London and North Western Railway Directory, to join in the opening celebration of the Bedford branch. About two o'clock the train left Bletchley, and a very pleasant journey was made back to Bedford. The excellence of the arrangements was generally remarked, and particularly the improved mode of laying the rails, whereby the least possible vibration is caused to the carriages in their transit.

'On their return from Bletchley, the travellers were delighted to see waiting at the station, her Grace the Duchess of Bedford, who was anxious to do honour to the party assembled, by gracing it with her presence; as well as to testify the great interest her Grace took in the completion of a work she had so auspiciously commenced – a work so important to the town and county of Bedford, with which her noble family is so intimately connected. Her Grace expressed her extreme satisfaction with all she saw around her; and it gives us great pleasure to add, that with the kindest consideration requested to be specially introduced to Mr. Jackson, the contractor, to convey to him her Grace's congratulation upon the successful completion of his contract . . . . Her Grace, in company with Mrs. S. Whitbread, Miss Whitbread and Miss Payne then retired to the refreshment room which was tastefully and elegantly arranged by Mr. Brashier, who in his usual admirable style, had provided, by order of the directors, a most excellent dejeune. Champagne having been handed round, the Duchess took the opportunity of proposing success to the Bedford Railway, to which all the ladies present most cheerfully responded.

'Her Grace having desired to see the preparations for the dinner to be given to the party at the Bedford Rooms, then retired for that purpose, and, having viewed the whole arrangements was extremely pleased, and conveyed the hope to Mr. Elger, who accompanied her Grace that the party might pass off with every enjoyment . . . .

THE DINNER

'At 3 o'clock a party of upwards of 200 persons . . . sat down to a splendid dinner at the Assembly Room, in Harpur-street, where there

was a profusion of turtle, game and almost every other luxury of the
season, and it was served up in the best possible style by Mr. C.
Higgins of the Swan Hotel . . . After the company had done ample
justice to the dinner, the Rev. Dr. Mountain said grace. T. J. Green,
Esq., the Chairman of Directors, presided, supported by H. Stuart
Esq., M.P., A. Sharman Esq., the Mayor of Bedford, the Rev. Dr.
Brereton, H. Littledale, Esq., Robert Newland, Esq., John Astell,
Esq., Robert Lindsell, Esq., Chairman of the Leicester & Bedford
Railway Company, the Rev. B. C. Smith, M. Prendergast, Esq.,
the Recorder of Bedford, Sir Harry Verney, Bart., the Chairman of
the Oxford & Bletchley Company, – Tootell, Esq., Director of the
London & North Western Railway, Capt. Huish, etc. etc. The Vice-
chair was ably filled by Theed Pearse, Esq., the Secretary of the
Bedford Railway, supported by Dr. Witt, T. A. Green, Esq., Thos.
Jackson, Esq., the contractor of the works. Thomas Barnard, Esq.,
and Isaac Elger, Esq., acted as Vice-chairmen at the long tables on
either side of the room. Henry Bruyeres, Esq., the able director of the
locomotive Department of the London & North Western line, and
Mr. Long, the intelligent assistant secretary, were also of the party.

'The Chairman gave the toast of The Queen, which was loyally
received. He said they had never had the light of the royal coun-
tenance in Bedford, and why? Because hitherto there had been no
railway (hear, hear). Who would care to come to a town without a
railway (hear, hear and cheers). Now, however, they had a railway,
and perhaps Her Majesty in the course of the royal progresses, would
delight her loyal subjects in Bedford, by paying them a visit . . .
The Chairman then said "The next toast I am about to propose to you
is one which your attendance today assures me will meet with your
cordial acceptance: it is a sentiment which I am sure throbs in every
bosom, and, I trust, will find utterance on every lip – Success and
Prosperity to the Bedford Railway (cheers). First, allow me to express the heartfelt gratification my brother directors and myself
experience at the sight of this magnificent assembly, testifying not
only your kind feelings toward ourselves, but the warm interest you
take in our great undertaking, for great it undoubtedly is; though
small in geographical extent, great in the results which must flow
from it – great in the benefits which it will confer (hear, hear). It is
now eleven months since our railway commenced; in that interval
has been performed, I may say, the work of years, with an efficiency
which does infinite credit to the contractors, and with an order and
propriety of conduct on the part of the workmen engaged, which has
been highly satisfactory to the country around. At that time many

mists hung round our undertaking, many doubts and difficulties were in our way; – now, those doubts and difficulties have been dispelled, the mists have vanished, and the horizon is clear on every side (hear, hear).

'At that time we had two formidable antagonists on either flank – the Midland & Eastern Counties Company on the north, and the Oxford & Cambridge on the south, either of which would have materially damaged our cause; they are now happily *hors de combat*, peace be to their manes. At that time our ally – the Oxford & Bletchley Company, the next most important link in our chain – was but a project, it is now a great fact, having received the sanction of the legislature, thus forming a continuous line from Bedford to Oxford under one management. It is true that our Cambridge Extension Line fell through in the last session on account of an engineering blunder; but that which seemed a loss is in fact a gain, for the project will be renewed in the ensuing session by the powerful Eastern Counties Company, with far greater chances of success, and a far more evident necessity for its allowance than before existed . . .

'As members of the vast commercial empire we know the great advantages arising from the cheap and rapid interchange of agricultural produce, the minerals, and the manufactures of different parts of the country, with the prosperity and happiness that result from it. And as members of this enlightened community, we must feel how the cause of morality is advanced, how science is promoted and how society improved by the quick and easy communication thus afforded between all its members . . . I now heartily call upon you to drink – Success and Prosperity to the Bedford Railway (loud and long-continued cheers).'

Of the local people who attended, T. J. Green, the Chairman of the Bedford Railway, was a prosperous Bedford coal and wood merchant, with an estate at Pavenham; the Member of Parliament, H. Stuart, lived at Kempston, and was related to the Stuarts of Tempsford; the Rev Dr Brereton was Headmaster of Bedford School; H. Littledale was at Kempston Grange, John Astell of Everton and Moggerhanger; Dr Witt lived in Potter Street (now Cardington Road), and was a former mayor of Bedford; Isaac Elger of St John Street, Bedford, a surgeon.

It is evident that the navvies had behaved well during the construction of the railway and belied their reputation. It is therefore pleasing to record that they were also feasted, as we learn from the *Bedfordshire Times* of 28th November 1846:

'We omitted last week to mention that on Wednesday Mr. Jackson, the contractor of the works, regaled the workmen employed at the Bedford Terminus. The supper was provided by Mr. Austin of St. Leonards Farm, which is more generally known as the "Old House at Home", and consisted not only of good old English fare, roast beef and plum pudding, but the table was supplied with game and other delicacies, stranger to the palates of the assembled *gourmands*. Mr. Mitchell, the superintendent of the works, presided and Mr. Scott the sub-contractor of the brick laying ably supported him as vice. It was a strange contrast to see 63 hearty fellows assembled in jovial carouse and reflect that some centuries back, the same room was used by the monks of St. Leonard. After the men had done ample justice to the viands, Mr. Mitchell in a manly speech proposed the health of Mr. Jackson, the response to which made the walls of "St. Leonard's" tremble, and certainly if, as is reported, any unearthly visitants dwelt therein their ghostships must have awaked from their reverie.

'The health of Mr. Randle and the other gentlemen engaged upon the works having been drunk, the same compliment was paid to Mr. Mitchell, the police at the terminus, host and hostess etc. Time being called, the men left, preceded by a band of rather a novel composition, we should say, to Jullien's ear, viz. one drum, one tambourine, one violin and three fifes. To the credit of the men, not one was intoxicated, although ample opportunity was afforded.'

It is not possible to cover the opening of every Bedfordshire line. The Dunstable Railway from Leighton Buzzard to Dunstable seems to have begun very quietly. The Great Northern attracted more notice. The *Bedfordshire Times* of 10th August 1850 has this paragraph:

'*BIGGLESWADE*

Opening of the Great Northern Railway. This event was celebrated with great rejoicing at this town. The day was ushered in by the ringing of bells; all the shops were closed, and everything betokened a general holiday. The Ampthill Brass Band was in attendance and paraded the streets. At 4 o'clock about 300 navvies were escorted through the town to a capacious tent where a substantial dinner was spread out. At 6 o'clock a large party consisting of the gentry of the town and neighbourhood sat down to a sumptuous dinner at the Town Hall.'

A leading article in the same issue described the run to Peterborough on a special train for the company's directors to view the line.

Bedfordshire had to wait seven years for the next ceremony, when the Midland Railway opened the line from Leicester through Bedford to Hitchin. On this, the first normal passenger train left Hitchin station for Leicester at 7.33 a.m. on 8th May 1857. The Midland paid £500 rent for the original facilities at Hitchin station, but this was increased to £60,000 when from 1st February 1858 they obtained running powers from the Great Northern for its trains to go on to King's Cross.

The opening day, 7th May 1857, was declared a public holiday in Bedford, and an excursion train left Hitchin at 7.30 a.m. calling at Shefford 8.00; Southill 8.15; Bedford 9.00; Sharnbrook 9.30; Welling-borough 10.15; Kettering 10.35 reaching Leicester at 12.00 noon. The *Bedfordshire Times* of 9th May 1857 described the day:

'*OPENING OF THE LEICESTER & HITCHIN RAILWAY*
This interesting event took place on Thursday under circumstances which will long be remembered by the inhabitants of Bedford . . . Shops were closed, streamers waved from buildings in different parts of the town . . . crowds of people were flocking to the station to secure their places several hours before the time fixed for the depart-ure of the trains. The Mayor, aldermen and councillors, assembled at the Shire Hall at half past 8 o'clock and accompanied by Mr. Barnard, M.P., several magistrates and other gentlemen walked in procession to the station, preceded by the band of the Bedfordshire Militia . . .

'The procession having arrived at the arrival side of the London & North Western station, no time was lost in taking possession of the carriages, and at a few minutes past nine the whistle sounded, the band, occupying an open carriage in front of those occupied by the town council, striking up a merry tune, and the train, numbering thirty-three carriages, first and second, started slowly on its journey . . . Several bridges, and each side of the line from Bedford to beyond Bromham-road were thickly studded with human beings waving their handkerchiefs . . . The Mayor and Corporation were met at [Leicester] station by Mr. Ellis, Chairman of the Midland Railway Directors . . . Shortly after the passengers of the first Bedford train were disposed of, the third class train came in sight consisting of 35 carriages . . . The first train left soon after 2, and arrived in Bedford at half past 4. The second train arrived about five o'clock.

'The Dinner took place at the Bedford Rooms, under the direction of Mr. C. Higgins of the Swan Hotel. About 174 sat down. W. W. Kilpin, Esq., (mayor) presided; supported by Sir George Osborn, Bart., the High Sherriff, J. Underwood, Esq., the Mayor of Leicester, T. Barnard Esq., M.P., S. Whitbread, Esq., J. Ellis, Esq., the Rev. J. Wing of Leicester, . . . Captain Polhill Turner and Captain E. Thornton . . .

'The Rev. E. G. Bayly [said] . . . The time for talking about the advantage of railways had long passed; the increase of population and increase of commerce had made England very great . . . Had Russia possessed the same means of communication . . . England might have been carrying on the war still . . . The advantages of rapid communication had been witnessed that day . . . many had been enabled to go 50 miles and back comfortably in time for dinner . . .

'The Mayor said "When the Bletchley branch opened the traffic brought to the town averaged 200 tons a month: the average was now 2,000 tons a month: coals 1,600 tons a month . . . The Midland Company was one of the most extensive in the kingdom . . . passing from Rugby to Derby, 57 miles; from Derby to Leeds, 74 miles; from Derby to Birmingham, 48 miles; from Birmingham to Bristol, 95 miles [and] several other lines making 333 miles, which give a total of 600 miles [and] lastly, from Leicester to Hitchin 62½ miles, making altogether a grand total of 662½ miles . . . The capital of the company is 21 millions. The staff list numbers 9,000 persons. [There are] 400 locomotives [and] 1,000 passenger carriages . . . The carriage he had the pleasure of riding in today . . . was one of the most beautiful he ever saw . . . There were also 10,000 carriages for stock and 10,000 for minerals." '

The Midland station in Bedford was not yet ready, and so the train started from St John's, the L.N.W. station. Not until 1st February 1859 did passengers begin to use the station we now call Midland Road. The journey from Bedford to King's Cross therefore had three phases. From 8th May 1857 trains from Leicester ran into and out of (St John's) L.N.W. station and passengers changed at Hitchin. From 1st February 1858 the trains continued to use the L.N.W. station but went through to King's Cross. At last on 1st February 1859 the Midland trains ceased to use the L.N.W. station and ran from the Midland (Road) station on the journey to King's Cross.

Something has already been said about the opening of the Sandy & Potton Railway on 9th November 1857. After Lady Peel had named the engine 'Shannon' there were the usual festivities. One report said that the dinner cost 2s 6d with an unlimited quantity of beer. The Market Square, Potton, was gay with banners, one reading 'Perseverance and Industry will join us with Cambridge'. Five years later Potton and Cambridge were indeed linked, when the little line was swallowed up in the Bedford and Cambridge Railway, though in the meantime the Great Northern branch across from Welwyn Junction to Luton and Dunstable had been opened with very little fuss. However, the *Bedfordshire Times* of 8th July 1862 contained:

'BEDFORD & CAMBRIDGE RAILWAY

We are informed that the new line from Bedford to Cambridge was opened on Friday last. A large train started from Bedford in the morning taking shareholders and other inhabitants of Bedford and the vicinity, free passes being issued by the directors . . .

'The agreeable manner in which the trains glide along and the comfortable style of the carriages are no mean recommendations in these days of general locomotion. At Blunham, the first station on the line from Bedford, the trip train on Friday stopped for the shareholders to make a brief inspection of the offices; the journey was then resumed and in a few minutes Sandy station reached. Here the line crosses the Great Northern Railway and then along the railway which was constructed by the later Captain Peel to Potton. Up to this point there was no demonstration on the part of the population living on the line, but the inhabitants of Potton turned out in great force to testify their delight at the success of a line of railway calculated to be of very great service to all classes. At this station there was a large influx of passengers, and the train then moved on through Gamlingay and Hatley, and at length reached Cambridge . . .'

The Bedford and Cambridge railway seemed to have completed the links that it was thought Bedford needed with the outside world. In the *Bedfordshire Mercury* for Monday 14th July 1862:

'Railway accommodation for Bedford may now be considered complete – Bedford now being intersected by excellent lines of iron road from East to West, and from North to South . . . Any part of the island can now be reached by the traveller with the utmost facility.'

However, building proceeded. In 1868 the new Midland extension from Bedford to London was opened. There was a ceremony but no dinner. This was partly because the Midland Railway had not been able to complete St Pancras station, and even more because they were stretched to the financial limit. They had opened services from Kettering to Huntingdon in 1866, to Manchester in 1867 and most serious of all was the enormous expenditure facing them to drive their line from Settle to Carlisle (opened 1876). As regards Bedford, the arrangement was for suburban trains to run from this town via Luton and St Albans to Moorgate Street as from 13th July 1868, while main line trains continued via Hitchin to King's Cross. When the great St Pancras station was ready on 1st October 1868 the main line trains and most of the suburban ones ran in and out of it, but a few trains still used the Metropolitan widened lines to Moorgate Street.

The *Bedfordshire Times* of 7th July 1868 carried this notice:

'*MIDLAND RAILWAY*
OPENING OF THE NEW LINE BETWEEN LONDON
AND BEDFORD THROUGH LUTON AND ST. ALBANS
FOR LOCAL PASSENGER TRAFFIC.

This railway will be open for local Passenger Traffic on Monday, July 13th, from which date the Midland Company's trains will run through between Bedford and Moorgate Street, calling at Aldersgate, Farringdon Street, and King's Cross Metropolitan stations. For Particulars of Train Service see Time Tables which may be obtained after July 6th at the Metropolitan Railway Stations, at any of the Stations between London and Bedford, or on application to the Chief Offices at Derby.

'Applications for Season Tickets to be made to Mr. C. Mills, Midland Agent, Great Northern Station, King's Cross, London. The Main Line Through Trains will continue to run to and from the Great Northern station at King's Cross until further notice.

James Allport,
General Manager.'

Derby, July 1868

The *Bedfordshire Times* leading article on 14th July ran:

'The official announcement of the opening of the Midland Extension Line from this town to London, already published in these columns, has been received by the inhabitants of Bedford, Luton, and the other towns along the line, with a satisfaction that only the removal of grave inconvenience of long standing could give rise to. It is difficult to imagine anything more annoying to business men than to travel between Bedford and Luton, for instance, by the circuitous route via Bletchley, Leighton and Dunstable, taking at least two hours and a quarter by a through train. We have known instances in which the journey has occupied even five hours, owing to unavoidable delays at the junctions above-mentioned. This want of adequate railway accommodation between Dunstable, Luton and Bedford has acted very prejudicially on the development of local commerce; and in addition to this we must mention the serious annoyances experienced by jurymen summoned to attend the Courts of Quarter Sessions and Assizes, many of whom have been fined for not being punctual in attendance. All this is now happily removed by the opening of the Midland Extension Line, and we have no doubt that a remunerative traffic, passenger and otherwise, will reward the exertions of the Company to provide railway facilities for the important district through which they have carried their extension line. The ordinary trains from Bedford are timed to reach Luton in 48 minutes, stopping at the intermediate stations of Ampthill, Harlington, and Leagrave. About 20 trains are to run each way on week days to and from Moorgate-street station of the Metropolitan Railway, calling at Aldersgate, Farringdon, and King's-cross Stations, to suburban and other stations on the Midland Railway, including St. Albans, Luton and Bedford. On Sundays it is proposed to run ten trains each way. The time-table will be found on our third page. Bedford, which was for a long time isolated from other towns for want of railway accommodation, is now, we are happy to say, one of the best served towns in the Kingdom and mainly through the enterprise of the Midland Company.'

More praise came from the *Bedfordshire Times* when on 21st July the new Midland station at Bedford was described:

'The station arrangements are most admirable, and the buildings of red brick and white stone facings have a very pretty appearance. In addition to the platforms in front of the booking-offices, waiting-rooms, and other offices, there is . . . a long platform, with one or two supplementary waiting-rooms and a signal-box, where one man has the entire control of the block signals . . . The table of fares appears to be very moderate.'

Public approval was complete with the opening of St Pancras station, the most beautiful in London. It is difficult to say which was the first train to run on the new line. If we mean the first passenger train of any kind, then it was the humble 7.35 all stations from Luton to Bedford on 1st October 1868; if we mean the first express to use St Pancras, then the 3 a.m. from Leeds arrived in St Pancras at 9.55 on that day. In the down direction the 10 a.m. Manchester express was the first, and it is convenient to regard this train as opening the service.

The L.N.W. had been operating the train service on the Bedford & Cambridge even before they took the line over completely. In 1871 the single line between Sandy and Cambridge was doubled, leaving only Sandy to Bedford (St John's No. 2) as a single track which it remained to the end. When the L.N.W.R. Chief Mechanical Engineer, the great Francis Webb, started the manufacture of steel rails at Crewe, they were tried out on the Cambridge branch, and at Blunham a new electrical apparatus was tried for the safer working of single line traffic.

The promised rail connection between Northampton and Bedford by a direct route at last became an accomplished fact on 10th June 1872. There was the usual rejoicing, but the official celebration was delayed until 26th July, because of the death of the Duke of Bedford.

On 3rd August 1872 the *Bedfordshire Times* contained the following account:

'*OPENING OF THE BEDFORD & NORTHAMPTON RAILWAY*
Banquet at the Assembly Rooms
On Friday afternoon 26th July the opening of this new railway was

celebrated at Bedford, a number of gentlemen from the counties of
Bedford and Northampton being accorded the invitation of Lt. Col.
Higgins of Picts Hill, Chairman of the Directors of the Company, to
a banquet which was held in the Assembly Rooms. The large hall
was effectively arranged for the occasion, and handsome decorations
in the form of a variety of greenhouse plants from the nurseries of
Mr. Sheppard being judiciously placed at the end of the room, and
on the tables and along the frontage of the gallery. The hall was also
carpeted for the occasion and flags were displayed from the front of
the building. The Chair was taken by Colonel Higgins who was
supported by the following gentlemen: The High Sheriff of Northampton Mr. Nethercote; the High Sheriff of Bedfordshire Mr. W. F.
Higgins; Colonel Gilpin M.P., the Mayor of Northampton Mr.
Marshall; the Mayor of Bedford Dr. Coombs; Mr. James Howard
M.P.; the Rev. Sir H. J. Gunning Bt. of Horton; Lt. Col. W. Stuart
jnr. of Tempsford Hall; the Recorder of Northampton Mr. Brewer;
Mr. G. Gunning; and Mr. Joseph Palmer. Other guests were Colonel
Cole, Cardington Mills; Mr. Charles Longuet Higgins of Turvey
Abbey; Mr. Harry Thornton of Kempston Grange; Mr. R. Orlebar
of Hinwick House; the Rev. G. F. W. Munby of Turvey; Mr. Henry
Allport; the Rev. J. W. Haddock of Clapham; Mr. E. Ransom of
Kempston; Mr. Carpenter of Kempston; Mr. Price; the Rev. W.
Suthery of Clifton Reynes; the Rev. C. C. Beatty-Pownall of
Milton Ernest; Messrs. A. E. Burch, James Pearse, W. Smail, M.
Whylley, W. J. Nash, H. Sharpin of Bedford; Mr. Stephenson of
Woburn; J. Garrard of Olney, Aldermen Bull, Jessopp, Sergeant,
Carter and Robinson of the Bedford Corporation, and Councillors
W. Harrison, Young, Sturges, Colburn, Lester, Wilson, Barrard,
Scoles, Roff, Roe, also of the Bedford Corporation, and T. W.
Pearse, Town Clerk. Caterer – Mr. Gunter of Belgravia, S.W., Band
of the Coldstream Guards under Mr. F. Godfrey.

'The Chairman regretted the absence of Mr. Charles Howard of
Biddenham due to the sale of his celebrated flock of sheep. Had he
known he would have postponed the gathering . . .

'In proposing the toast of the Bedford & Northampton Railway
the Chairman said, "In 1845 we had the Northampton Bedford &
Cambridge Railway – a Bill was procured, but all at once came one
of those peculiar panics which have happened in this country almost
periodically, and which put a blight on this undertaking. The concern was wound up . . . Then came the period of more recent date
when the new line was taken up. A Bill was introduced and passed
both Houses, but then came one of those unfortunate periods when

the money market got into a sinking state . . . In the course of two years there occurred a better state of things and we were enabled to enter into an agreement with that distinguished firm Messrs. Clark and Punchard. When I spoke of Mr. Whitbread I was lamenting that he could not have lived to see the accomplishment of the object he had so much at heart . . . I offer you gentlemen of Northampton the right hand of friendship (enthusiastic cheering)."

'The High Sheriff of Northamptonshire said in reply: "I recollect the coach between Bedford and Northampton of the days gone by which absorbed three mortal hours in accomplishing the distance and how long it might take that tortoise among vehicles – the carrier's cart – I don't pretend to say (laughter). One afternoon passing that carriage I said to myself:

'The way is long, the wind is cold,
The carriage is infirm and old.' (much laughter)." '

1. *Building the embankment of the London & Birmingham at Hillmorton, near Rugby, 1837, by Edward Rudge.*

2. *Excavating the Tring cutting on the London & Birmingham, by J C. Bourne, 1837.*

3. *Leighton Buzzard's first railway station, 1838.*

4. *St John's Station, Bedford, opened 1846, with train, circa 1870.*

5. *Lidlington Station, opened 1846, as it was circa 1890.*

6. *Sandy Station, opened 1850. People waiting to welcome wedding party, circa 1890.*

7. *The 'Shannon' engine built for Captain William Peel, for the Sandy to Potton railway, 1857.*

8. *Cast iron bracket with letters 'BC' (Bedford & Cambridge) at Potton Station, built 1862.*

9. *Bedford Midland Road Station with Kirtley engine, circa 1870.*

10. *Train leaving Sandy hauled by Webb 18 inch goods engine, circa 1900.*

11. *Market gardeners' carts outside Potton Station in the potato season, circa 1900.*

12. *Hat boxes ready for loading on Bute Street Station, Luton.*

THE ANNUAL
TEMPERANCE EXCURSION
TO THE
SEA-SIDE.

The Luton and District Temperance and Band of Hope Union have made arrangements with the GREAT NORTHERN RAILWAY, and intend running Special Trains to

YARMOUTH
AND
LOWESTOFT,
On Wednesday, July 6th, 1892.

SPECIAL TRAINS WILL LEAVE	A.M.	1 Day.	RETURN FARES. 3 and 4 Days.	6 and 7 Days.
LUTON, G.N.R.	6 30			
New Mill End	6 35	4/6	8/-	9/6
Harpenden, G.N.R.	6 40			
Wheathampstead	6 45			

Children under 12 Half Fares.

Day Excursionists return from Yarmouth (Vauxhall Station) at 8 p.m.; Lowestoft (G.E.R.) 8 p.m. Passengers for more than 1 Day return as per Co.'s Time Tables.

Parties of 8, by giving early notice to Mr. W. H. COX, can secure Reserved Compartments.

It is requested that an early application for Tickets be made to any of the following Gentlemen :—

Mr. W. ORD, 80, Chapel Street.
" J. GILLAM, 28, Windmill Street.
" J. GILTROW, 37, Havelock Road.
" W. WALSH, Jun., 9, George St. West.

Mr. J. DOCKRILL, Barber's Lane.
" H. BURNET, 54, Collingdon Street.
" F. STRATFORD, 34, Pondwicks Road.
" W. BRYANT, 6, Vicarage Road.

Mr. W. H. COX, 57, Waller Street.

The Committee recommend GOATES, 155, King Street, Yarmouth, for good accommodation on reasonable terms.

PLEASE LOOK THE OTHER SIDE.

GEORGE DALTON, Crown Printing Works, Cheapside, Luton.

13.   *Temperance excursion poster – Luton to Yarmouth, 1892.*

14. *Dunstable North Station showing Stirling mixed traffic engine on passenger train, circa 1900.*

15. *Johnson goods engine at Bedford Midland Road Yard, loaded with
Longhurst & Skinner's removal vans, circa 1900.*

CHAPTER 9

CONTRACTORS AND NAVVIES

'I have no fear but the work will soon be done. In that part of the country there are a great many men known by the name of "navigators" who have much experience in work of this description.' So spoke H. C. Lacey, Chairman of the Ely & Huntingdon Railway at the half-yearly meeting of the company held on 29th July 1845. These words are of interest because they show that the term 'Navigators' was coming into general use, soon to be shortened to 'navvies'.

An enormous number of workmen was needed to build a railway, and they were concentrated in a small area. When the line was finished, the men were turned adrift, and might live as vagrants until a new scheme was advertised, and this would seldom be in the same neighbourhood as the last. These figures give an indication of the scale on which work proceeded:

Total railway route mileage completed 1825–44	2,235
Total of new mileage completed by 1845 ..	2,523
Total of new mileage completed by 1846 ..	3,157
Total of new mileage completed by 1847 ..	3,870
Total of new mileage completed by 1848 ..	5,123

Hamilton Ellis, is his work *British Railway History* says:

'The engineering contractor was a new figure in British commercial life. With the coming of the railways the country saw the largest programme of heavy public works which it had known since the building of the great cathedrals and abbeys in the middle ages. The only thing which anticipated railway construction had been that of the canals, and from this stemmed the navigators, quaintly named for they had nothing to do with working any sort of craft – the navvies, the cream of British heavy labour and perhaps the most ferocious and voracious race of men to be let loose on the land since Cromwell produced his Ironsides. They formed the contractors' armies and the king of contractors was Thomas Brassey. The Grand Junction Railway gave Brassey his real start. One fact that emerged from Brassey's Grand Junction contract was his extraordinary ability to deal with the navvies. These wild men who were a law unto themselves, each of whom was reckoned to lift about twenty tons of earth a height of six feet in a day, whose staple food was beef, beer and spirits in enormous quantities, whose principal relaxation was gambling, whose dalliance was with polyandrous female camp followers, who lived "Box and Cox" twenty together, in turf hovels, followed and obeyed the gentle spoken Tom Brassey with the same sort of devotion as the Grande Armeé had given Bonaparte . . . Brassey loved them.'

The *Railway Record* was one of the early periodicals of the railway age. The first issue appeared on 13th April 1844 and by 3rd August it found itself obliged to say something about the navvies. In a leading article headed 'Railway Navigators' it says:

'The improvident habits of the class of men known as navigators are alluded to in a report to the Poor Law Commissioners appended to the fifth report of the Select Committee on Railways. It appears that, during the winter of 1842 as many as fourteen of these persons were admitted in one night into the Abingdon Workhouse. It is stated that they usually receive wages varying from 3/– to 4/6d for every ten hours' labour, but are required by their gang of fellow workmen to subscribe a gallon of beer daily and another gallon at the time the ganger or sub-contractor pays the wages. As the works approach completion employment is difficult to be obtained, and then the labourers, having previously spent their earnings in the most lavish manner, undergo the severest privations, frequently subsisting for a whole week upon the wages of a single day. Ultimately there is no longer any prospect of employment upon that particular undertaking and then the workmen remove, seeking shelter and food in the Union workhouses on their route, to some other locality where employment is more abundant.'

From the newspapers one has the impressions that Bedfordshire did not suffer unduly from the navvy invasion. Our first railway from Bletchley to Bedford, opened on 17th November 1846, was only 16 miles long, and so the labour force was small. However, between that date and 10th June 1872, when the last railway (Northampton to Bedford) was opened, there were occasional incidents.

In 1854 the Midland Railway was extending their system, and building the line from Leicester through Bedford to Hitchin. The contractor for the work was the great Tom Brassey, but as the army of navvies moved into the county, it is easy to understand that some concern was aroused. The following is an extract from the register of the Michaelmas 1854 Quarter Sessions Minutes:

'In consequence of the great number of workmen employed in the works of the Leicester & Hitchin Railway which intersects the County from north to south, ORDERED, subject to the consent of one of Her Majesty's Principal Secretaries of State, that the number of constables first appointed under the Act of 2 & 3 Vict. c. 93 be increased by one additional constable to act during the ensuing half year, and that application be made by the Clerk of the Peace to the Secretary of State for his consent as required by the second section of the same Act.'

There were, too, many accidents, as we see from the minutes of the board of the Bedford Infirmary, dated 1st January 1855:

'The Secretary having reported that several very severe accidents have been received from the Leicester to Hitchin Railway now being made it was RESOLVED that Mr. Brassey and Mr. Knowles the contractors be applied to for an annual subscription or donation to the Infirmary and that representation be made to them of the heavy expense which such cases are to the Institution.'

If several were injured, fortunately few were killed. The Coroner's register of inquests has only one entry at this time:

'27th December 1856, Richard Street, navvy age 26, Killed at Souldrop.'

Another leading contractor was Samuel Morton Peto, and from his books a comparison can be drawn as regards the wages paid to navvies just about the time the Bedford Railway was built, and again when the Midland Railway extended their line from Bedford to London:

	1843	1869
Mason	21s	27s
Bricklayer	21s	25s 6d
Carpenter	21s	24s
Navvy	16s 6d	18s

Railway construction continued in the county on and off between the years 1857 and 1890. Scarcely had the last beer bottle been thrown away on the completion of the Midland Railway's extension from Leicester to Hitchin in 1857, when the sound of the pick and shovel was heard in the south of the county. However, the event which affected Bedfordshire the most was the building of the main line from Bedford to London, linking the county town to Luton and St Albans directly for the first time. The line attracted general interest, and three views in F. S. Williams's *The Midland Railway* show scenes in Bedfordshire near the line: Elstow Church; Dallow Farm, Luton; and a view of the countryside just to the south of Luton. Two tracks only were laid and the engineering works became more difficult as the line progressed toward London. Liddell and Barlow had surveyed the route in 1862, and the undertaking was so extensive that it had to be awarded to four contractors. From Bedford going south, A. W. Ritson and Joseph Firbank were selected to carry out the works, and nearer London the contracters were Thomas Brassey and Stephen Ballard. At Ampthill the tender submitted by John Knowles of Shefford was successful and he was awarded the contract to build the first (eastern bore) tunnel. Knowles was experienced in tunnel work, but nevertheless two of his men were killed during operations. One was overwhelmed by a fall of earth and another, Charles Bell of Luton, aged 65, was run over by a contractor's wagon.

With the opening of the new trunk line to London on 13th July 1868 there was a brief lull until the construction of the Northampton & Bedford line. The route had been surveyed twice in 1864, by Charles Liddell and by Sir Charles Fox. Liddell's line, with small variations, was the one finally built. When the work was put out to tender, the contract was awarded to the contractor Harrison, but as the weeks went by he showed no inclination to sign the papers and finally he withdrew. The work was then offered to the firm of Waring Bros who had done so well on the main line to St Pancras. They at first agreed, but later withdrew. The line involved some heavy earthworks, but nothing which could really have daunted such an able firm. Finally Clark & Punchard agreed, on 25th May 1870, to do the work, and the first train ran on 10th June 1872. Although this was the last new railway to be opened in Bedfordshire, the navvies remained.

There was intense competition between the various companies, and the Midland became aware of the fact that the London & North Western Railway was planning to lay quadruple track from Euston to Roade. The idea was to give a separate road to the coal trains, and to leave one line free for passenger trains. In 1872 the Midland secured Parliamentary powers to widen the line between Rushton and Bedford, and further powers were granted in 1876 for more detailed work just north of Bedford. The engineer was J. S. Crossley in both cases. This meant a return of the navvy, but by now public opinion could no longer accept the conditions in which he lived.

Charles Magniac of Colworth, a magistrate and Member of Parliament, brought the matter before the Quarter Sessions. The report in the *Bedfordshire Mercury* of 7th January 1882 reads:

'A NAVVY ENCAMPMENT: WYMINGTON

Mr. Magniac said that he should like to mention a matter which had some connection with the Police Committee business. At his end of the County the owners of property were at the present time practically at the mercy of bands of navvies who are employed on new works in that neighbourhood by the Midland Railway Company. These navvies take possession of any part of the adjacent property which they choose, and go about in bands of 18 or 20 with guns or dogs, breaking down fences, taking railings off, and, as a matter of course, poaching, but of this he did not wish to say anything. The damage, however, which they do in his own neighbourhood was becoming very serious indeed and very considerable. He made no complaint whatever against the police; on the contrary he had great pleasure in expressing now, in the presence of Col. Josselyn [the Chief Constable], the appreciation with which the efficient performance of their duty by the police was regarded by the inhabitants of the locality, for the police do their utmost to protect property. The state of things at Wymington was a perfect disgrace to a civilised country. From 300 to 500 navvies are gathered and encamped upon a swamp, with green water lying in holes and ditches in front of the houses or huts of these people, and not the slightest attempt had been made by the Company to introduce sanitary arrangements or to make religious provision for those people. Such a thing did not seem to have entered into the minds of the Company, and the amusement of the boys and many of the men was to assault the clergyman who went amongst them and to disfigure the building which some gentlemen had erected there in order that divine worship might not be neglected. For himself, he would bring the matter before the Directors of the Midland Railway Company, but it was a disgrace to a civilised country to see men, women, and children, numbering altogether from 300 to 500, huddled together in a space of 2¼ acres. The misery of the worst Irish cabin was nothing compared with the state of things amongst these people. Only yesterday he tried to see about a man who had been seriously injured, but the state of filth and mud was such that it was impossible for him to get there. The medical attendance also was complained of. The fact was that these people were brought there and as much work as possible was got out of them, but as to their moral or religious comfort it was far from the thought of the Company . . . Poaching he would say nothing about, but the damage done to property, to the fences and hedges, was so great that when stock are taken out into the fields they stray all over the country.

'Mr. Barnard asked on whose property are the cabins built.

'Mr. Magniac said that part are built upon land taken by the Railway Company for the purposes of their traffic, and part are upon a small field which has been leased from a proprietor of land in Wymington parish . . .

'The Chairman asked if Mr. Magniac suggested an increase in the number of police in that locality.

'Mr. Magniac replied in the negative. Such a step would have no appreciable effect. He hoped the Court would excuse him for trespassing so much, but the fact was that the condition in which these people are placed renders it impossible that they could do anything but stray all over the place. The filth and dirt of the place where the houses are situated was so excessive that not only did he not prevent these people from going on his land but actually encouraged them. It was hardly to be expected that they would spend an hour in that filth if they could get anywhere else.'

The result was that Quarter Sessions 'RESOLVED that the Chief Constable be instructed to put himself into communication with the Midland Railway Company and the Sanitary Authority of the Wellingborough Union respecting the condition of the huts used by the navvies employed in the Midland Railway works at Wymington, and the conduct of the navvies.'

Newspapers for the two following years disclose nothing further, so we must presume that conditions improved. In 1893, when the second (west) tunnel was bored at Ampthill, the men included five hundred miners from Lancashire. By the end of the century railway expansion had ceased, and quiet once more descended on the countryside.

CHAPTER 10

TRAVELLING BY RAIL

When once the speed had been accepted and the cheapness realised, train travel became the accepted means of moving about the world, but some people took a little time to trust the new devices. The London Brighton & South Coast Railway had opened their route to Portsmouth in June 1847 but this did not attract Mrs Hester Dawson (*née* Gery) who wrote to Mrs Hester Wade-Gery of Bushmead on 4th December 1847: 'Have taken lodgings at Portsmouth; have seen Ada and Freddie. Little Henry was tired. I came in the coach which rattles very much but not nearly so much as those vile cars.' Another member of the family had the opposite opinion. W. H. Wade-Gery wrote to his parents on 30th November 1847:

> 'Will come to see you and Mary Hannah on Saturday next. I shall take a day ticket by the ¼ before 10 o'clock from Bedford and be at Ramsgate in the evening, return on the Monday morning.'

The 9.45 from Bedford (L.N.W.) reached Euston at 12 noon. Mr Wade-Gery would then take a cab to London Bridge for Ramsgate. The South Eastern Railway had built the line in 1844. A train journey in 1847 would seem spartan to us. Mr Wade-Gery would arrive at the (St John's) station by horse-drawn vehicle and might have to wait while his paper ticket was written out by the booking clerk. Edmondson's invention of printed cardboard tickets (1839) had not been universally adopted by 1847, and until then the clerk booked you in his book of paper tickets. From the low platform it would be quite a step up into the four-wheeled vehicle, lighted, if first class, by an oil lamp. This was a November day but there would be no heating in the carriage. If he had a good deal of luggage, much of it would be strapped on to the roof. At the head of the train would be a diminutive 'Bury' engine which would jerk the train into motion as all the carriages were loose coupled. The short coaches would clatter over the wrought iron rails, which only 20 feet in length would give a bumpy ride. The time of thirteen minutes to the next station, Marston, would seem agreeably fast, as the distance of six miles gives an average of 28 m.p.h. and the maximum was probably nearer 40. No smoke would be seen as the engines consumed coke fuel. The stop at Marston would be effected by the fireman and the guard each screwing down a hand brake. The loose coupled coaches would come together, the shock being diminished by buffers stuffed with horsehair. The ascent from Lidlington to Ridgmont would be slow, after which good speed would be made to Bletchley where arrival was timed for 10.26. If the platform road was not clear a policeman in frock coat and top hat would signal to the driver to stop just as he does today on the road. Although signalmen have replaced policemen for over 100 years, they are still referred to as 'bobbies'. If the platform were clear, the train would draw in, leaving our friend time for a cup of coffee before the London train arrived.

Even the elderly often preferred rail travel to coach for long journeys, since it was far less tiring. C. Haedy, the Duke of Bedford's Agent-in-chief in London wrote to the Woburn steward on 23rd May 1839, when Bedfordshire's only link was the Leighton station of the London & Birmingham, opened the previous year.

'I am exceedingly sorry to hear of poor Robert's misfortune, and I fear it is not unlikely to be attended with serious consequences. He appeared to have come very ill provided with Information . . . He had been, as I understood him, to the Woburn Coach Office, but had refused to go by the coach, on understanding he should have to go between forty and fifty miles . . . As he . . . seemed disposed neither to return back to Cornwall [nor] go by the Coach, I advised him to go by the railway to Leighton and there hire a Gig or chaise-cart or any other conveyance, by means of which I told him he might get to the Abbey and see Mr. Hitchins that evening, and he set off with the Intention of doing so. I gave him a direction . . . and sent the office Porter with him, who paid for his place (with Robert's money) and saw him safe to the carriage, and gave particular Directions to the Guard to look to him and see that he was set down at Leighton. I thought him a very old man to be sent so great a distance. I asked him if he wanted any refreshment, but I understood him to say that he didn't and he said he did not want any money. I hope he will not have a serious illness.'

It isn't clear how Roberts had become ill – possibly he became confused and lost his way when he arrived at Leighton – but he had been sent for from Cornwall to work on the grotto which the 6th Duke was having built at Woburn.

Two years later, in July 1841, the steward at Woburn wrote to Haedy on a matter of much greater importance, for the Queen was to visit Woburn, and extra police were being sent down from London for the occasion.

'The four Policemen can start on Monday morning by the six

o'clock train, get over from Leighton, refresh themselves and be with me by ten o'clock (or eleven would do) to get their assistants assigned to them, and the places for their stations pointed out.

'When you see the Duke about the regulations for lookers on, will you also consult him as to the procession, viz. as to order in which the Queen is to be received – the road to the Abbey, whether by the Basin Pond and West Front, or the Back Road – and the *pace* at which to travel – some of the Cavalry will be rather heavy.

'I expect we shall muster about 150; I have confined the request of attendance to the Tenantry who entirely or for the chief part get their living by the Duke's estate, this is the Farmers, and have made the distinction between those and the people holding only accommodation land etc., but there is some difficulty as regards the house tenants in Woburn, and therefore I have said that those who have horses and like to join us may, those who have not horses or cannot ride are not expected to put themselves out of the way. It is thus left an open question.'

A Colonel Cavendish wished to buy a horse from the Duke, and so Haedy wrote from London to Charles Burness of Park Farm, Woburn, on 26th April 1845: 'The Duke of Bedford wishes you to send the black filly to meet at Leighton the train which leaves London at 11 o'clock on Monday morning, and which I believe reaches Leighton at about half past twelve. A person from Colonel Cavendish will meet it there at that time and will decide whether it will suit or not.' The filly did suit, and the reply said 'the gentleman has taken her with him'.

An amusing scene is created by a letter from W. Grant of Harrow Road, London, to a Leighton Buzzard solicitor. Grant had been asked to sign the text of the Leighton Buzzard enclosure award, a large heavy volume, about 2½ feet by 2 feet. Grant said that he was travelling north by a train that would stop at Leighton.

'June 1848

I intend coming down by the train that arrives at Leighton at 33 minutes past one on Wednesday, so if you will be at the station with the Award and a pen and ink ready I will sign it. I shall probably be in a second class carriage. I do not intend staying at Leighton beyond the time of the train's delay.'

Much later, we find Anthony Trollope using Leighton Buzzard station. In his autobiography he mentions that after returning from Australia in 1872 he sent three horses from his house at Waltham Cross, Essex, to stables at Leighton Buzzard. He used to travel down by an early train from Euston, and ride to the meet from Leighton Buzzard, and so get in some hunting, which he loved. We are not, therefore, surprised to find at least one of his heroes doing the same thing.

The new method of travel gave rise to a new etiquette which is referred to in several journals of the time. The *Bedfordshire Mercury* in its issue of 23rd March 1861 has this to say:

'The Higher etiquette proper to be observed in railway carriages forms a most important part of this subject. It is not alone sufficient to avoid treading on a fellow passenger's toes, or sitting on his hat, or incommoding him with gusts of wind from the open window. The social amenities of railway intercourse should embrace many acts far more thoughtful and unselfish than these, and opposed to the first come, first served principle which governs so many travellers. It is very delightful for two or more intimate friends to be able to retain the whole compartment to themselves during a long journey without paying the Company for that luxury, but they should not grasp at this unfair privilege by filling each seat in their carriage with portmanteaus and rugs or by acting the old rather exploded game of the lunatic and his keepers. They should not attempt to block up the carriage windows at the side of the platform nor should they commit themselves so far as to say that several seats are engaged by passengers who have just gone to purchase a newspaper. Such tricks are sure to be exposed by some determined station superintendent before the starting of the train, and they often lead to unpleasantness. The travellers who are forced into such carriages by the arm of authority are not likely to prove very agreeable companions on the journey, while the greedy firstcomers can never remove the impression caused by their deliberate lies. The soft seat in such cases becomes hard and unbearable, and the carriage is turned into a cage, a round house or a dungeon.'

The *Bedfordshire Mercury* (24th August 1861) reported that on the Paris, Lyons & Mediterranean Railway experiments were being carried out to provide some heat in carriages. 'Waste steam' from the engine was circulated through pipes, the coaches being connected by india rubber tubing, and the temperature in the first class was said to reach 60° Fahrenheit. At this period first class passengers in England were given footwarmers which were metal containers filled with hot water; ten years later the London & North Western Railway brought out a footwarmer containing acetate of soda which generated heat after a porter had given it a good shake-up. It was not until 1874, thirteen years after the report of the experiments in France, that the Midland Railway introduced the Pullman coach, and we find the beginning of the modern method of steam heating pipes supplied from a boiler.

Some of the county's early travellers kept diaries. One was the Reverend R. A. Williamson of Kempston Manor. His father had been rector of Campton and the family was well-to-do. The diary covers both the years before railway travel was general, and the railway age, and allows an interesting comparison between horse and rail transport.

'28th May 1840. Posted down from town to . . . Kempston fare (Barnet to Kempston)	£4	6	3
15th June 1840. Trevor's carriage took us to station at Leighton to meet the "train". Gave coachman and footman		7	6
Arrived Euston 9.20 leaving Leighton 7.30.			
13th August 1840. "Fast train" [on London & Southampton Railway] to Winchester. fares . . .	£1	15	0
Reached Winchester at 2 p.m. ½ hour after time. Reached "station" at 5¼ but train was again late . . . started not before 6. fares		5	0
Reached Southampton in 20 minutes [13 miles]			
15th July 1842 [Paddington] for the mail train ¼ [to] 9, fare	£1	7	6
Started at 9, reached Bath 20 [minutes] before 1			
10th August 1842 Two Railway guides (Bradshaw) . . .		2	0
11th August 1842 Two 1st class fares to Leeds . . .	£5	4	0
From London thro' Rugby to Derby and Leeds in less than 9 hours			
15th August 1842 Fares from Leeds to York (2) 1½ hours		12	0
28th September 1842 Coach fare from Alnwick to Darlington . . . 64 miles, by mail, ¼ [to] 8 to 3½ . . .	£1	0	0
Railway fare from Darlington to London in first class carriage, 3½ to ¼ [to] 5, 13½ hh. [231 miles] fare . . .	£3	8	0
Stopped ¾ h. at York, crossed ferry to see Cathedral 1 [hour] Letter at Newcastle . . .			4
Stopped ½ h. at Derby, cup of tea			6
Stopped 10 m. at Wolverton, a bun			1
2nd January 1844 Set off [from Bath] 9 for Sutton Coldfield [by coach] 2 inside and 1 outside places to Gloucester	£1	14	0
[Saw] Cathedral at Gloucester from 1 to 2		1	0
Railway Gloucester to Cheltenham		3	0
Biscuits at Station			6
Fares, three in [side coach] from Chelt. to Birmingham, 2¾h. [fare] . . .	£1	16	0

Carriage, Birm. to Sutton . . .   17 0

9th November 1844 Trip with A. and L. to Colchester, started at 8½ from Shoreditch, Colchester at ¼ [to] 11, fly to Greenstead, Hithe . . . seeing St. Botolph's priory, St. John's Gate [and] Castle . . . Started home at 6 and reached Shoreditch at 8½, home at 9.

18th December 1844 Down to Sutton [Coldfield], by 9 o'clock train: great bustle and crowd: second engine required: detained 40 [minutes]: fares (each)   £1 5 0
Soup at Wolverton 1/- did not make up our lost time, Birmingham at 2.

24th April 1845 [In London] by water with A. and others to see model of new atmospheric railway: much pleased with it: simple and intelligible . . .

5th August 1845 Guide Book for Birmingham Railway   3 6

[4th January 1846 Married Anne Grey]

21st January 1846 . . . Started in Mr. T's carriage for Leighton: found that only a 3rd class train went at 5, and we had to wait till 7 – walked about the town, tea at ¼ [to] 6   5 6

15th August 1846 . . . to "George & Blue Boar", to reach the Bedford Times coach . . . travelled outside . . . reached Shefford safely [fare for 2]   £2 1 0

[16th September 1846 Times coach Bedford to London 5½ hours]

15th March 1847 . . . In the little carriage to Tamworth at 6¼ a.m. thence by railway to Derby, York, Darlington and Stockton, in second class to save the difference for the Irish (this was 29/-) . . . to see Robert at Stockton [fare for 2]   £3 11 3

[Robert was going to the Cape as a Bishop]

19th May 1851 [Worcester] to London [to see Great Exhibition] [three tickets on Great Western Railway]   £4 5 6'

The eleven years of travel end here. The Reverend R. A. Williamson was headmaster at Westminster School, and on 8th September 1851 was installed as Hon. Canon of Worcester Cathedral. He died in 1865. The journey to Colchester in 1844 shows that day trips were by now possible, and he visited the Great Exhibition six times.

Another Bedfordshire diarist was J. T. Brooks of Flitwick House. Both he and Mr Williamson were men of substance and both discovered that it was possible to make long day trips by train, returning to their own beds at night. J. T. Brooks is a family man travelling mostly to London, whereas Mr Williamson, having places where he can stay in Kempston, London and Sutton Coldfield, travels further afield, and if there is no line of railway on his route, does not hesitate to hire expensive horse conveyance. The diary of J. T. Brooks covers only the year 1843. Brooks has to make the journey from Flitwick to Leighton Buzzard, the nearest station:

'13th January 1843 At 5 o'clock a.m. dearest Johnnie and George left us on their return to Town. They rode to Leighton for the 7 o'clock Train and arrived in Town soon after 9 – a horrid ride – dark as pitch – very heavy rain and sleet and yet (from the frost of last night) the Roads so slippery the Horses could with the greatest difficulty be kept up. Bob Adams sent to the Station (at 2 a.m. he started from here with carpet bags) to bring the Horses back. A disagreeable day – miss our dear Lads whose company we have enjoyed much the last fortnight.

26th January 1843 . . . dearest Johnnie came home today – sent the carriage for him in the morning to Leighton and he arrived there at ½ past 3 and reached home at ½ past 5, quite well thank God.

1st February 1843. Rose early, left home this morning at a quarter past 9 a.m. (our time) and proceeded (at half past 8 a.m. real time) in the carriage to the Leighton station (for the Train at 20 minutes before 11). Reached London 20 minutes before 1. *A miserable morning* [Johnnie was going to Portsmouth for India]

3rd February 1843 [At] one o'clock I took a cab to the Railroad [in London]. . . . At half past one the train started and reached Leighton at ½ past 3 where the Carriage was waiting and arrived at home at half past 5 o'clock (6 o'clock our time).

17th March 1843. Rose at half past 4, breakfast at five, and at half past 5 (five by the real time) left home for the Leighton station, to take Mary Ann to Town on a visit to the Williams and other friends. Got to Williams . . . (Guildford Street) at ¼ past 9 o'clock . . . Left for home by the 6 o'clock train from Euston Square. Got to Leighton at 8 where I found the Carriage waiting . . . and got home at 10 o'clock. Very cold coming home.

[Thursday 11th May 1843. Trotter and his family (with us for 24 years) left by Ellis and waggon to go to New Zealand]

13th May 1843. Rose at 4 o'clock a.m. (half past three by the real time) and at quarter past 5 set off in the carriage (accompanied by dear Willie) for the Leighton station. Reached London . . . at 10 minutes past 9. Trueman Tanqueray also accompanied me; we three got into a Cab and went to . . . Guildford Street. [They went to the British Museum to see the Elgin Marbles and mummies, then to the National Gallery and Burlington Arcade, Piccadilly. Then by carriage to the Horticultural Gardens at Chiswick, where there was a band of the Coldstreams and Grenadiers. They left Turnham Green at ¼ past 4, and arrived at Guildford Street at 5.10, cost 16s.] Got to the Railroad at 10 before 6, went to Leighton (Mary Ann, Willie, I and Tanqueray) in the first class, having come from it in the 2nd class. Arrived at Leighton at 5 minutes before 8, and home 5 minutes before 10 (25 minutes after 10 by our time) after a very pleasant day, the cost . . . being £3 10 6, but it was a treat for all the children . . . The day was fine and no rain.

24th May 1843. Rose at 4 a.m. at 5 started for Leighton station and got to London at 9 . . . Breakfasted . . . Walked to the Fete of the Botanic Society in the Regents Park – enjoyed it very much . . . equal to the Chiswick – walked to the station at 6 (40 minutes) got to Leighton at 8, home . . . thank God! at 10.

25th May 1843. At home all day.

15th June 1843. Left home at ½ past 8 (eight by the real time) got to Leighton at ½ past 10 (10 by the real time) for the Train at ¼ past 10 and got to town at ¼ past 12. After luncheon walked in Regent Street.

Sunday June 18th – evening to St. Pancras [church] service . . . splendid.

30th June 1843 Returned . . . by 6 o'clock train got to Leighton at 8, home at 10.

19th July 1843 Spent a delightful day in London. Left at 5 returned at 6.

13th October 1843. Went to Town . . . to bring home Mary Ann . . . Rose at 4 o'clock, started at 10 minutes before 5 o'clock a.m. in the carriage to Leighton, for the train at 10 minutes past 7 . . . Reached town at 10 minutes past 9. Breakfasted with the Williams . . .

15th November 1843 Rose at ¼ before 4 o'clock a.m., at ¼ before 5 a.m. set out to Leighton for ¼ past 7 train.

6th December 1843 Rose at quarter before 4; breakfast at half past four. Set off in the carriage for Leighton – quarter before five arrived at Leighton before 7. Arrived in Town 10 minutes past 9.

7th December. Euston Square 6 o'clock. To Leighton at 8 o'clock and home at . . . 10 o'clock.'

The phrase 'our time' obviously means that the clocks at Flitwick were kept half an hour fast.

The great protagonist on the railway scene in Bedfordshire in the 19th century was W. H. Whitbread, and Southill station was opened in order to serve the Southill estate. As the mansion and park are most attractive, many excursions were organised to visit the park, for this was the age of the great railway excursions. On Friday 21st June 1861 several corps of rifle volunteers assembled in Southill Park at the invitation of Mr Whitbread for drill. According to the *Bedfordshire Mercury* the men left by the 2.25 p.m. train from the Midland station. A heavy rain continued throughout the afternoon, but after having partaken of refreshments the men gave three cheers for Mr Whitbread. The bands then struck up and the men marched back to Southill station. On 17th July 1866 a great fête was held at Southill Park, and 2,000 passengers travelled from Bedford station. Another passage from the *Bedfordshire Mercury* reads:

'On 18th August 1868 the teachers of Bunyan Meeting Sunday School and a few friends numbering 53 proceeded by the 11.58 train from Bedford to Southill station, tickets having been issued at single 2nd class fare for the double journey. The party proceeded to the Park by the kind permission of S. C. Whitbread Esq. and were conducted through the beautiful gardens. Tea was prepared on the banks of the lake.

'Innocent games were indulged in and then came a stroll to Warden church. The party returned on the 7.39 train to Bedford having enjoyed the rural picnic exceedingly.'

The total number of railway excursions advertised in the *Bedfordshire Times* and the *Bedfordshire Mercury* is enormous. One is given below, and others are to be found in Appendix E1 and E2.

'*L.N.W.R.* Excursion. London to Edinburgh, Glasgow, Dublin, Wales, Liverpool, Chester, Birmingham, etc., etc.

Monday July 1st or 8th 1850, offering a choice of 9, 12 or 15 days.

London to Edinburgh or Glasgow and back		...	42 0d
,, ,, Dublin	,,	...	42 0d
,, ,, Bangor	,,	...	28 0d
,, ,, Windermere	,,	...	32 6d
,, ,, Liverpool or Manchester and back		...	21 0d
,, ,, Shrewsbury & Chester	,,	...	20 0d
,, ,, Leeds & Huddersfield	,,	...	25 0d
,, ,, Birmingham	,,	...	12 0d

ENCLOSED CARRIAGES

Thus affording an opportunity at a small cost of visiting the Highlands, Dublin, and the romantic lakes of Killarney, North Wales and its charming scenery; the greatest wonders of the world – the Britannia and Menai bridges and Conway Tube; Snowdon, the Vale of Llangollen, the ancient City of Chester, Eaton Hall the magnificent seal of the Marquess of Westminster, the lakes of Cumberland and Westmorland, the Isle of Man, the manufacturing districts of Lancashire and Yorkshire.

Monday July 1st at ¼ before 6 punctually, returning to London on or after July 10th.'

We have referred above to the awkward journey from Luton to Bedford before 1868, which caused the following entry in the Bedfordshire Quarter Sessions minute book for Midsummer 1861:

'Mr. Smart presented an estimate of the comparative expense of the conveyance of prisoners by the Turnpike Road or by the Railway from Luton to Bedford. There appeared to the Committee no question as to the matter of expense – the Railway affording the cheapest mode of travelling, but the change of rail and the return of the constables has hitherto presented the greatest difficulty. Mr. Smart has, however, entered into a correspondence with the General Manager of the L.N.W.R. which he will lay before the Court on Tuesday next. Mr. Smart will also be prepared to lay before the Court the comparative expense of sending prisoners by the above railway, or by the branch line which communicates with G.N.R. from Luton.'

Timetables show that if the constables and prisoners caught the 7.25 a.m. from Dunstable, and then changed at Leighton Buzzard and Bletchley, they would arrive in Bedford at 10.15.

Although the Midland trains were running direct to Hitchin in 1857 to connect there with the Great Northern, this was in competition with a horse-drawn bus which ran between Bedford and Sandy. A notice in the *Bedfordshire Times* of 7th November 1857 reads:

'A bus leaves the "Red Lion", High Street, Bedford daily at 7 a.m. reaching Sandy in time to meet the up train which arrives in London at 9.30. Returns to Bedford on the arrival of the Parliamentary train leaving London at 6.30 a.m.

'Leaves Bedford again at 1.45 p.m. to meet the mixed train due London 5.30 p.m. Returns to Bedford on the arrival of the 1.45 p.m. train from London, due Sandy 3.20; arrive at Bedford 5 p.m.'

When the Bedford to Cambridge line was opened in 1862 it was supposed to provide a connection at Sandy. Presumably by that time the horse bus had disappeared, but it seems that the new train services left something to be desired. The letter quoted below appeared in the *Bedford-*

shire Times on 22nd July 1862 (shortly after the opening of the Bedford and Cambridge Railway) and it is very much to the point:

'Is the Cambridge line intended as an accommodation of the public? If so they must arrange their timetable and keep such time as their trains will meet certain ordinary trains on the Great Northern. I had anticipated the 8.5 train would meet the down Parliamentary train from London due at Sandy at 8.28; and so it would, had more energy and punctuality been shown on leaving Bedford. Being 8 minutes behind time on starting the consequence was I lost the "Parly" and had to return to Bedford, disappointed at the cheapest mode of transit to the North. Lest any other unlucky wight should be caught in the same trap, I write this as a caution.

VIATOR'

Reference has been made to the pioneering in luxury travel by the Midland Railway in 1874. On 21st March of that year, three new Pullman cars named 'Midland', 'Excelsior' and 'Victoria' went from St Pancras to Bedford and back for a trial run. The passengers were directors and friends and lunch was served on board by Spiers & Pond. The experiment was considered successful, and on 1st June a Pullman car was added, as a regular feature, to the 8.30 a.m. from Bradford reaching St Pancras at 2.05 p.m. Generally you bought refreshments at the stations. The *Bedfordshire Mercury* of 15th April 1876 contained a complaint from a hungry traveller, and since the Midland station had a refreshment room which always received favourable mention in the local press, the station referred to must have been the L.N.&W. (later St John's).

'I do not know who is to blame but certainly travellers who find themselves called upon to stop at Bedford station are in a somewhat sorry plight as far as refreshment is concerned. Possibly by roaming round the neighbourhood all that could be required might be obtained, but at the station itself not a bun or a glass of lemonade is to be had.

'Surely there is sufficient energy in the town to establish a refreshment room of some sort so that travellers may not be compelled to regard Bedford as a likely spot in which to be.

STARVED OUT'

A coffee stall was opened in the station yard at St John's from 1940 to 1949, but this seems to be the only period when any facility was available.

Last, we come to the 'Dickens Episode' which produced a good deal of correspondence, and refers to the involuntary stop which the famous

writer made on Bedford station in 1867. The train which Dickens caught –
the 9.35 a.m. from Leicester, was one of the fastest trains of the day in
1867. It ran without stopping to Market Harborough, a distance of 16·15
miles in 24 minutes, an average of 40·4 m.p.h.; the next stop was Bedford,
the time for the 33.1 miles being 45 minutes, giving an average of 44.1
m.p.h. The speed from Irchester to Sharnbrook summit would have been
quite low owing to the gradient of 1 in 120, but once 'over the top' the
driver would take advantage of the falling gradient of 1 in 119 and his
speed would rise to 60 or 65 m.p.h. A Kirtley express engine of the No.
100 class could have done so easily. If he had been delayed at stations or
by signals he would certainly try to make up time. (Modern diesels
exceed 90 here.) The most likely explanation of Dickens' conduct is that
his nerves were in a bad state. He had had a miraculous escape from death
when his train was wrecked at Staplehurst on 9th June 1865 and it is often
suggested that he never really recovered and that his death on 9th June
1870 was hastened by this harrowing experience. A brief account of the
Staplehurst episode will enable us better to appreciate Dickens' appre-
hensiveness. He was travelling from Folkestone to London by 'The Tidal',
that is to say, a train whose departure varied daily according to the time
of high tide in Folkestone Harbour. The train took passengers and goods
off the packet boat, and of course it was the arrival time of the boat which
governed the running of the train. John Benge was foreman in charge of
a gang engaged in renewing the timbers of a bridge over the River
Breult near Staplehurst, and he planned to do part of the work between
the passing of the 2.51 up train and the 4.15 down. He knew there was
'The Tidal' but he had misread his working timetable and thought it
passed at about 5 o'clock. This was sufficiently unfortunate, but he then
acted in a most negligent manner. He knew that the regulations stipulated
that a look-out man should post himself 1,000 yards from the scene of
the operations, having clipped a detonator to the rails every 250 yards as
he walked. Benge told the man to walk only 500 yards and not to use any
detonators. He then proceeded to remove two lengths of rail and the
wooden baulks below, when he heard 'The Tidal' in the distance. The
man posted at 500 yards did his best to warn the driver, but the inadequate
brakes of the period did not permit the driver to stop in time. The train
plunged into the river below the bridge, and Dickens was badly shaken.
He got out of his carriage and helped those who were injured. Later he
wrote to a friend 'A perfect conviction against the senses that the carriage
is down on one side comes upon me with anything like speed.'

Two years later came the Bedford incident. On 5th February 1867 the
Bedfordshire Times published a letter from Mr Andrew Wright referring
to earlier correspondence which had appeared in *The Times*, and in the

same issue of the *Bedfordshire Times* was a long leader much of which is quoted below.

'A ride in a Midland Railway fast train has so operated on the nerves of our good friend Mr. Charles Dickens that he determined to pull up at Bedford, wait for a slower train, and write to *The Times*. His letter which was published on Tuesday and the discussion it has provoked will no doubt produce good results if there is anything wrong. Mr. Dickens wrote as follows:

"As it is better to prevent a horrible accident by a timely caution than sagaciously to observe after its occurence that anyone acquainted with the circumstances out of which it arose could have easily forseen it, I beg most earnestly to warn the public through your columns against the morning express on the Midland Railway between Leicester and Bedford.

"I took the train this morning leaving Leicester at 9.35. The reckless fury of the driving and the violent rocking of the carriages obliged me to leave it at Bedford rather than come on to London with my through ticket. When we stopped at Market Harborough general alarm was expressed by the passengers and strong remonstrances were urged on the officials, also at Bedford. I am an experienced railway traveller at home and abroad; I was in the Staplehurst accident; I have been in trains under most conceivable conditions, but I have never been so shaken and flung about as in this train, and have never been in such obvious danger.

"The very obliging authorities suggested that the road was 'rough' from the thaw and that I was in a light carriage. As to the first suggestion, I am certain from experience on other railways since the thaw set in that there is no such roughness on other railways. As to the second, one of the passengers who protested the most strongly was a gentleman in a heavy carriage next to my own. I may add that my companion in the carriage (who left the train with me) is most certainly constantly on English railways and fully confirms what I have here written (January 26th)."

'To publish the whole correspondence from *The Times* would occupy too much space and therefore we give a summary of the chief suggestions offered. Fear is as contagious as the small pox. A number of persons begin now to share the nervousness of Mr. Dickens, who is probably by them regarded as a high authority on railway matters since his last work on "Mugby Junction". Accordingly there are letters from several persons who have passed through the dangers of a ride by express on the Midland Railway. A "Captain R. E." felt the oscillation but his alarm was qualified by his wit and logical reasoning, and he came to the conclusion that the fantastic dance of a drunken character which the carriages were performing could not be accounted for except for the fact that they were in the "Shires" and that the presence of some pink coats and tops in the train might possibly have sent the carriages mad on that pleasant hunting morning. "A Shareholder" followed suit by declaring his belief that the unpleasant oscillation was due to the reckless driving of the express train, and that it is always so when he goes by it. The "Another Traveller on the Line" says that the express rolls and tosses on the Midland Railway but runs smoothly on the Great Northern Railway although at an increased pace. From the general tenor of his letter we glean that an alleged rocking arises from some defect in the permanent way. Then a Mr. G. C. Masters, who says he is a regular traveller on the same line daily, and that Mr. Dickens who is described as the above well-known individual is probably but a casual, adds his testimony that the speed had become "frightful" and that the oscillation was so great that we were rocking about scarcely able to keep our seats. He thinks there are two considerations; that which other correspondents appear to anticipate, *viz.* being killed by a smash on the line, and one which he suggests is nearly as bad "being frightened to death". Mr. W. P. Collins writes to say that Mr. Charles Dickens is right. He adds that the Company drive their light carriages with reckless fury and he is careful to avoid the Midland Railway expresses. Somebody else says that this is not a regular mode of procedure of the expresses and thinks the oscillation complained of might have been caused by the thaw altering the level of the rails. Mr. Alfred Ellis travelled by the train of which Mr. Dickens complains, read one of his books all the way in great comfort, and felt neither rocking nor shaking. He thinks that Mr. Dickens' discomfiture was "due to the imperfect coupling of the carriages and not to the condition of the road". Mr. James Howard of Bedford, who uses the same train very frequently writes as follows:

> "I have read with surprise Mr. Charles Dickens' account of the perils of the Midland Railway. I constantly travel by the morning express referred to, which although very fast, runs as smoothly as any I have ever journeyed by. I am an experienced railway traveller like Mr. Dickens having travelled in three-quarters of the globe. The line from Leicester to Hitchin is considered by engineers one of the best pieces of permanent way in the kingdom. I have been a constant traveller on this

line since its opening, and never having met with the slightest
accident, I think it is only due to the Midland Railway Company
with which I am entirely unconnected to assure the public that
Mr. Dickens' experience is very different from mine and that
they are as safe on the Midland Railway as on any line I am
acquainted with."

'Mr. M. T. Bass writes that for his sins (we presume he means
political sins) he has to travel some 7,000 miles in the course of the
Session on the Midland Railway, principally between Leicester and
London. He has given formal notice to the Company's servants of
their liability for bumping their passengers about in the express
trains. Probably the Company will think this complaint about speed
by Mr. Bass as somewhat ungrateful, for if we mistake not, this
gentleman at one time brought charges against the Directors at
General Meetings for not taking him up to London fast enough.
Mr. J. F. Halford testifies that the express trains run a portion of the
way at a rate of 60 m.p.h., but that although they have done so on
this line for many years there has not been the slightest accident.

'There is much to be said on both sides. Many persons like to go
fast and the Midland Railway Directors try to oblige them. In doing
so they give them a little more shaking than if they take them gently
along by the slow trains . . . It is curious when one knows the persons
who compose the Midland Railway Board of Directors, to hear
them charged with recklessness, furious driving and generally being
"too fast". The public expect to go at the maximum speed, and
demand that the trains shall keep time, and in such a case must
endure a little more rocking than they would have by slow trains . . .

'We have understood that all persons employed by this Company
are well paid and therefore the line should be well worked. The
Directors will be benefited by the discussion, and the public will
receive a greater assurance of safety when the real cause of the
oscillation has been ascertained. Mr. Dickens has so far, done good
service by his letter and we hope his next visit to Bedford will be
taken under more agreeable conditions.'

CHAPTER 11

ACCIDENTS

Railway accidents never fail to command attention, partly because of their comparative rarity (contrasted for example with road accidents) and partly on account of the massive damage which ensues. An express train in rapid motion possesses a kinetic energy which is frightening in its proportions, and is hardly matched in its destructive power. At first there were few accidents as the railway was little more than a line from A to B and trains were few and widely spaced, but as the system became more complex and trains multiplied in numbers, so did the number of accidents increase. The first locomotives were feeble enough, and the attention of the engineers was concentrated on obtaining more power. The braking of trains was of secondary importance. The method used on road vehicles was adapted, that is to say a train was brought to a stand by the friction of a block of wood against the iron tyre of the locomotive or vehicle. The pressure on the block was increased by a lever, and later more so by a wheel. The normal points of braking were the locomotive tender and the brake van at the rear, helped by brake vans marshalled in the train if necessary. Obviously, braking power was governed by the strength of the operator. In the 1840s and 1850s the number of collisions due solely to inadequate braking power caused engineers to seek some improved method, but another fifty years were to elapse before the ideal – continuous automatic brakes – was to be evolved.

Personal injury on the railway can be divided into two classes (1) accidents to fare-paying passengers arising from a mishap to the train in which they are travelling, and (2) the less spectacular, but no less tragic, accidents to persons crossing the line or straying on to the track for one reason or another.

The absence of accidents on the early railways gave rise to the following eulogy in the *Railway Times* of October 1840:

'The superior safety of railway travelling over that of any other system is established. For example on the London & Birmingham, which was one time dragged before the public more than any other Company for its management, the travelling from September 17th 1838 since it was opened throughout to August 31st last, has been no less than 81 millions of miles, and there have been carried 1¼ million of passengers with but a single fatal accident. It is true that there have been a few cases of contusion, but only one serious, and one case of simple fracture.'

Equally enthusiastic was the coroner of Southall who had fifteen miles of the Great Western and fourteen miles of the London & Birmingham in his district. 'During the period 1838 to 1845', he reported, 'I have not held a single inquest. During the same time several inquests on passengers by stage coach have been held – a fact which showed the superiority of railway travel.'

Unfortunately these halcyon days were to come to an end because the very success of the railways resulted in mushroom growth and a far greater density of traffic. The Railway Mania burst upon the country in 1845 and in that year 288 route miles of railway were constructed, to be followed by 634 in 1846 and 712 in 1847. There were two bad accidents in 1847, the first being at the Dee bridge on the Chester & Holyhead Railway, when a cast iron girder broke, tipping the passengers in the leading coaches into the river. Three were killed and sixteen injured. Later that year the tyre of an express engine on the Great Western broke into pieces at Southall, and two drovers travelling in a cattle train on an adjacent line were struck and fatally injured. These misfortunes so preyed on the nerves of Catherine Welby, that she wrote to Mrs Wade-Gery of Bushmead Priory on 1st July 1847:

'Returning by Derby, Northampton and St. Albans to London, now a much better road to traverse than the old North one for accomodation as I found no want of horses and the Inns well kept and arrived the second day after quitting [her sisters] at 6 o'clock. One of the drivers who had the day before conveyed the Duchess of Sutherland, told them there was no doubt but the posting business will be again revived. You may easily believe what joy to my cowardly heart such news was, and I think not less to yours, as I hope after these last two fatal accidents you will no longer venture your Life to such fragile chances, particularly as every year it will be more dangerous all things having been built by contract that alone endangers the case . . .'

Miss Welby's fears were not unreasonable, for avoidable accidents continued to occur for the next forty years. Improved materials and methods of inspection went a long way towards reducing the number of boiler explosions and derailments, but it was the human element which was the principal factor in causing disasters, chiefly because points and signals did not interlock, trains were not worked on a space interval system, and brakes were weak and unreliable. The Board of Trade inspectors, capable men drawn from the Royal Engineers, issued reports after each serious accident emphasising the necessity for 'Lock, Block and Brake.' They meant, of course, interlocking of points and signals, train movements by the block system, and automatic continuous brakes. As the companies were slow to act, Parliament finally tired, and by a series of Acts, notably the Regulation of Railways Act 1889, forced the companies to improve their methods. Often, railway managers spoke of 'interference' by the Board of Trade, and no doubt some boards of directors with an eye to profits, considered the cost of adopting all the precautions would be greater than that of settling claims and repairing damage after an accident. Although there were fifty-three serious accidents between 1847 and 1890, conditions improved considerably in the 20th century, when it could be said that the safest place in Britain was the inside of a railway carriage. Thus as recently as 1964 British Rail carried nearly 1,000 million passengers without a single fatality.

Turning now to accidents on the railway involving members of the public, excluding passengers and workmen, records show that there were thirty-nine inquests on persons killed on the Bedfordshire railways during the thirty-three years from 1854 to 1886. In the early days it is evident from local newspapers that people had not become accustomed to the new high speed of the trains, high that is, in comparison with horse-drawn vehicles. On Monday 28th January 1861 at 7.30 a.m., George Chappel, a platelayer on the Great Northern Railway was making his usual walk along the track between Luton and Dunstable examining chairs and rail joints, when he discovered the body of an old man lying in the 'four foot'. He carried the body to *The Balloon* public house where an inquest was held by Mr Ezra Eagles junior. The victim was Richard Gibbons, who when refreshing himself in that same public house on the previous day, had informed the landlord that he had just had an eight mile walk. Obviously he was healthy enough, but in the semi-darkness of the January morning he misjudged the speed of the train. In this case there was no evidence of alcohol taken to excess, but the same cannot be said of James Cherry, brickmaker of Biggleswade. He entered the *Brick-makers' Arms* public house at 7.30 p.m. on Saturday 23rd March 1861 and drank heavily for two hours. Staggering out of the inn, he made the fatal decision to take a short cut across the Great Northern main line. As he had not arrived home, a search was made early on Sunday morning and the body found near the railway. Despite the fact that Cherry had contributed to his own death, the jury strongly recommended that the G.N.R. should 'adopt means in the future to prevent trespassing on the rails'.

Two years later, at Sandy, drink again seems to have been responsible for a fatality, which happened on the occasion of Sandy Feast. James

Brittain, aged 26, was determined to do justice to the feast for there was an extension of drinking hours. At two o'clock in the morning his friend George Ball happened to meet him near *The Stone Axe* and seeing his helpless state, tried to persuade him to go home by way of the common. Brittain's obstinacy increased, and he closed the conversation by saying 'I'll see you damned first'. Well after midnight George Smallcombe, driver of the mail train, was about 1½ miles from Biggleswade and Thomas Putman, the fireman, thought the engine had struck an object but he did not say anything to Smallcombe until they arrived at King's Cross. The driver immediately examined his engine and what he saw made him notify a station official. In the meantime, John Walden, guard of the following train had seen an object on the line near Biggleswade and had stopped his train. The coroner's jury returned a verdict of 'Accidental Death'.

Deafness could be a contributory cause, because a train coming up-wind is quite noiseless and can trap even people with keen hearing. Possibly that is why Susan Jackson, aged 26, who was crossing the Great Northern main line near Arlesey Siding station early one March morning was knocked down and fatally injured, despite the frantic cries of Mr Walters, the stationmaster. She seemed to hear neither train nor voice. Mr Whyley, the deputy coroner, agreed with the verdict of 'Accidental Death', when the inquest was held at the *Lamb Inn*. When John Bates, labourer, 55 years of age, was killed near the same spot the following year (1865), the jury, on learning that about 800 people crossed the line daily, recommended that the Great Northern Railway should erect a footbridge.

In the case of Thomas Hanger the weather played its part. He was walking to Biddenham when he called at the *Barley Mow* in Bromham Road for three pennyworth of gin and water. It being a cold snowy night, he asked for another, but six penn'orth of gin and water cannot be regarded as out of the ordinary. At 11.30 p.m. warmed by the fire, he set off for Biddenham but made the fatal decision to walk partly along the railway. He had already been struck by one train when the driver of a down goods train passing Bedford just after midnight saw an object lying in his path and found it quite impossible to stop his train before running over the object. Footmarks in the snow showed that Hanger had crossed the line once and had then changed his mind. It was on the stepping over the rails for the second time that he met his death.

However, one inquest shows clearly the difference between then and now. To be poor in the 19th century was to be poor indeed. On 28th July 1861 John King, a builder living in Shefford, saw a man whom he took to be a tramp wandering about the town. In the early hours of the following day the poor wretch was killed by a Midland goods train near

Henlow. His name was never found out, and at the inquest, which was on an unknown man, evidence was given as follows:

John Joyce, who was the fireman on an engine between Shefford and Henlow on Tuesday morning said 'I am a fireman in the employ of the Midland Railway. At 4.25 I saw a man kneeling on the left hand line . . . he seemed to drop. The laff guard of the engine caught him'. (Joyce must have said 'life guard' which today is called a 'guard iron'.) P. C. Reuben Pepper said that he had searched the clothes of the deceased and had found an empty tobacco box, two short pipes, two crusts of bread, part of a boiled potato, no money and two pieces of old newspaper. The inquest did not determine why he died. There was no doubt in the case of James Spring of Sandy, who was charged with 'casting and throwing himself on the line of rails of the Great Northern Railway when a train was due and expected, with intent feloniously wilfully and of his malice afore-thought to kill and murder himself on 6th July 1877'. Spring was arrested before the train arrived, but subsequently was found not guilty and discharged.

Not all accidents were tragic, and for this reason one to a passenger in the 3.40 p.m. Euston to Birmingham express is worth relating. On Monday 23rd January 1871 a young man was travelling alone in a second class compartment when, near Leighton Buzzard, the floor of the carriage suddenly dropped out. He sprang up on the seat, and leaning out of the window, tugged at the communication cord which ran to the guard's van. He said that he heard the bell ringing but the train went on. One or two floor boards, in contact with the rapidly rotating wheels, emitted sparks and splinters and 'jerked about like parched peas in a frying pan'. At length the train slowed down and the young man jumped out without waiting for it to stop, fortunately without injury. His hat and luggage had fallen out with the floor and were found considerably the worse for wear on the track at Leighton. On another occasion at Wolverton, some wagons containing pig carcases were shunted on to the main line by mistake, as the points leading to the siding had been left open. The 5.30 p.m. Liverpool to Euston express ran into the wagons, splintering them and scattering pork all over the tracks. Willing hands gathered the meat off the lines, and many families in Wolverton dined off roast pork.

So far, the recommendation by the Board of Trade inspectors for the universal adoption of 'lock, block and brake' was meeting with little response. Interlocking would have prevented the approach of the express while the siding points were open. Continuous brakes would have avoided a collision. The Midland Railway had already equipped a train with a new invention – the Westinghouse brake, and on 10th April 1874 a Midland train fitted with this air brake ran to and fro, experimentally, between

St Pancras and Bedford. Unfortunately the brake was not adopted, partly because of disputes between George Westinghouse and certain British railway companies. Thus by 1880 the Midland Board had still not made a decision on the fitting of automatic continuous brakes, and again we find the Bedford to London line the scene of brake trials, this time with Barker's non-automatic vacuum brake, which turned out to be ineffective.

It is remarkable that only two serious accidents occurred in Bedfordshire during the period covered by this book, and in only one could speed be regarded as the relevant factor. In the other the proximate cause was a signalling defect.

The Bedford Accident, Friday 12th March 1875

When the Bedford Railway was opened in 1846, the signalling system then common in England was adopted. A signal had been placed opposite where St John's No. 1 signal box is today, and this signal was intended to be the up starting signal for Bedford. Normally the semaphore arm is located at the end of the station platform, in which position it can more closely control the movement of trains. The disadvantage of the Bedford up starting signal was that, even if at danger, a train could move forward as far as the signal. This was of comparatively little importance between 1846 and 1857, but in the latter year, the Midland Railway extended their line from Leicester to Hitchin, crossing the L.N.W.R. tracks on the level. Rail and road crossings on the level are a nuisance, but when rail crosses rail on the level, danger is added to inconvenience. The Bedford starting signal was now in a position which invited an accident, as a train which stopped in obedience to the signal would stand foul of the Midland lines. However, the L.&N.W.R. made no effort to alter the position of the post. It became the accepted practice at Bedford for a train to wait in the station platform (always referred to as the London platform) until the starter signal was lowered.

On 12th March 1875, the 7.15 a.m. train to Bletchley was standing in Bedford station. The driver received the 'right away' from the guard who had not troubled to see if the signals were 'off'. Although John Perkins was familiar with the road and knew the procedure at Bedford, he unaccountably moved the train forward towards the signal. As he crossed the Midland line he was alarmed to see a green Midland engine and its train of crimson lake coaches speeding towards Bedford. The *Bedfordshire Mercury* relates:

'The signal at the crossing was against the L.&N.W. train, the signalman having lowered the signal for the 6.45 a.m. from Hitchin to cross to the Midland station. As the signal was clear, the driver of the Midland train was coming at his normal pace, but when near the bridge on the Elstow Road, he saw steam rising from the engine of the L.&N.W. train, and thinking this could not be right, he shut off steam as he came through the bridge, and at once applied his brake. Though he did all in his power to avert a collision, and the North Western driver hurried on, the Midland engine caught the last carriage of the L.&N.W. train broadside and went completely through it. The North Western carriage was shivered to splinters. The occupants of the smashed carriage were the Rev. William Sprott of Glasgow, 45, Charles Wilkins, 32, a bricklayer of Bedford, and Mrs. Stimson also of Bedford. Of those seriously injured, the Rev. Mr. Sprott was decidedly the most so. A stretcher was fetched from Britannia Ironworks on which the reverend gentleman was conveyed to the Infirmary; the man Wilkins also. Several persons saw the accident happen and the alarm was given to the Midland and London & North Western stations. A telegraphic message was sent to Bletchley for a breakdown gang. The L.&N.W. train proceeded to Bletchley at 7.45.

'The Midland train sustained little damage; the passengers were uninjured but the engine was derailed. By dinner time the lines were clear. The signalman Bishop is confident as to signals and said to our reporter – "Why, our driver was wrong, the signal was against him. A porter on the L.&N.W. station says the signal was against Perkins".'

Unfortunately Mr Sprott died and at the inquest the signalman, Richard Bishop, said that when he saw the L.&N.W. train going against the signal he ran with a red flag, but the driver was on the left-hand side of the engine. (On most railways the driver stood on the right, but on the L.&N.W. he was on the left.) Bishop also said that the Midland train was travelling at 6 m.p.h. and the L.&N.W. train at 12 m.p.h. at the time of the collision. James Warren, station master at the L.&N.W. station (it was not called St John's until 1924) said that a bell was rung to indicate that the duties at the booking office were completed and the foreman then told the guard he could go. Captain Tyler, the Board of Trade inspector, said that both the L.&N.W. and the Midland signals were on the wrong side of the crossing, and had not been altered since 1857. The verdict at the inquest was one of 'Manslaughter against John Perkins'. He had been dismissed from the railway service after the accident, and was now arrested. Perkins appeared before the Bedford assizes on 26th July 1875 and pleaded, in mitigation, that sleet was falling at the time of the accident. He was fined £20. It is interesting to note that Perkins was defended by the Associated Society of Railway Servants of which he was a member.

One unusual point emerged at the inquest and that was that both drivers were named John Perkins.

The main reason for the accident was the negligent placing of the L.&N.W. signal, but if better brakes had been fitted to the Midland train, the driver could have stopped before the impact. G. P. Neele, superintendent of the L.&N.W.R. in his book *Railway Reminiscences* states that his company was at fault, and that the signal was moved to the end of the up platform (its present position) soon after the accident.

The Arlesey Siding Accident, 23rd December 1876

The year 1876 had begun badly for the Great Northern Railway. On Friday 21st January, there had been a double collision at Abbots Ripton caused by one of the worst blizzards in the records of the time. The G.N.R. had used semaphore arms working in slotted posts and the slots had become filled with snow, preventing the correct aspect being displayed. In December came a somewhat similar accident.

Saturday 23rd December 1876, was a day of biting cold, and the afternoon became prematurely dark with heavy clouds and snow flurries. The 2.45 p.m. express to Manchester was waiting to depart from King's Cross. The competition for Manchester traffic was very keen, and only picked men were found on the Manchester express engines. On the day in question the driver was Thomas Pepper, a man with twenty-five years of excellent service behind him. His mate was George Smith. Pepper left the terminus promptly, but the engine was inclined to slip on the wet rails. The slipping proved troublesome, and by the time the train had passed Potters Bar summit, it was several minutes late. Therefore after Potters Bar Pepper opened the regulator wide. There was a slight rise at Woolmer Green, but thereafter the gradient would be favourable to well past Hitchin. The train would be travelling at 65 m.p.h. at this point.

At Arlesey Siding station (later called Three Counties) a pick-up goods train of twenty-five wagons had arrived from Peterborough. The driver had to attach some more wagons standing in the western siding before going on to London, and this manoeuvre involved crossing the down main line. It was already 3.30 p.m. but Graves, the signalman, unwisely decided that there was time for the goods train to reach the siding before the express was due to pass. He kept the down distant and home signals at danger, and felt safe with this slight protection as the signal lamps had just been lit. If all had gone well, the operation would have been foolish, but as things turned out it was more than foolish. As the train was crossing over to the down line, three wagons became derailed, and Walters the station master frantically summoned some platelayers to assist in re-railing the vehicles. They had just decided that the task was impossible when the distant roar of an express was heard. It was then that they realised that they were to be witnesses of a terrible accident. On the engine, Pepper had been running under clear signals for mile after mile, when, to his surprise and consternation, he saw the red eye of the Arlesey Siding distant signal. This meant that the home signal was also at danger, so he immediately shut the regulator and whistled for the guard to apply the brakes in his van. Smith had already screwed down the tender brake with all his might. But at such a speed the train slid forward on the slippery rail and soon the home signal came in sight, and what was worse, a goods train sprawled across two roads. Pepper told Smith to jump, but he stayed on the engine until just before the collision when he also jumped. He landed on his head and was killed outright. According to the *Bedfordshire Mercury* the engine jumped over one wagon before embedding itself in the next, and five coaches were wrecked. Monk, a railway policeman, went at once to the signal box to have 'obstruction danger' sent by telegraph to the neighbouring boxes. Walters asked for the breakdown train to be sent from Hitchin and for another from Peterborough. He also sent messengers on horseback to Biggleswade for doctors. By 10 p.m. on Friday the up line was cleared, and the down line by the same time on Sunday. The fatally injured were Thomas Pepper, driver; John Lovell; Abigail Longstaffe of Dulwich, passenger; Lucy Thompson of Grantham, passenger; Maurice Mitchell of London, passenger.

Captain Tyler presided at the Board of Trade enquiry on the accident, and Mr Graham, a Secretary of the Amalgamated Society of Railway Servants was also present. The former deplored the type of brake fitted to the G.N. trains, and he thought that this railway's method of operating the block system was most unsatisfactory. When an express is concerned, it should be signalled several block sections ahead. As Graves decided not to accept the express he should have blocked 'back' to Hitchin, so that the train could have been held there. Both accidents show how right were the Inspectors of the Board of Trade to insist on the interlocking of points and signals; the division of the line into block sections with one train only in any one section at a time; and the necessity for automatic continuous brakes.

Originally the control of the movement of trains was by the time interval system. If several trains were waiting to start, one would be despatched and then after an interval of five or ten minutes, the next would be sent out. If a train stopped through engine failure, then there was nothing to prevent the second train from colliding with the first, unless a railway policeman gave a warning signal. Even then the crude brakes would not always stop the second train in time. Railways therefore began to evolve a better means of control based on a space interval. This was known as the 'Block System' because a line of railway was divided into block sections each under the control of a signal box. The system should mean that only one train is in one block section at a time, which ensures maximum safety. Sections can be many miles long in the country, and only a few yards at a busy junction; although in the latter case there may be modifications, yet the basic principle remains the same.

Growth has been gradual. To replace the railway policeman we find the London & Croydon Railway using Gregory's semaphore signals in 1841. Two years later, the South Eastern Railway began to use interlocking near Bricklayers' Arms. This means that when signals are lowered to permit a train to pass, other signals which might permit conflicting movements are locked in the danger position by mechanical means. About this time the first explosive detonator was used on the rail to warn a driver in foggy weather that his signal was at danger. Further improvements were made when equipment became reliable. For example, the L. & N.W. Railway used the electric telegraph between Wolverton and Tring as early as 1849, and it was useful when a train carrying the Prince Consort travelled up from Northampton.

Signalmen were still, however, having to run some distance from one lever to another, which could be dangerous, particularly in fog or at night. In 1861 the Eastern Counties Railway adopted the idea of grouping the levers in one frame, which is the beginning of the modern type of signal box. The Board of Trade Inspectors were becoming interested in signal interlocking, especially when an accident occurred which would have been prevented by such a device, and in 1873 the Inspectors started to put pressure on the railways to interlock all junction levers. Another step forward was made in 1874 when W. J. Williams of the London Brighton and South Coast Railway invented the notched 'distant' signal which could be passed at danger, but which indicated the position of the next 'stop' signal, thus giving the driver much more space in which to stop his train. The notched arm showed red at night, the same as the stop signal, which could be confusing, so in 1908 the Metropolitan District Railway introduced the yellow arm and yellow light at night. This obvious advantage became general from 1925.

The Regulation of Railways Act (1889) compelled all lines to adopt 'lock and block', i.e. the interlocking of points and signals in signal boxes, and the movement of trains under the block system. In 1892 the Board of Trade required all semaphores to have counterweighted arms to ensure a positive return of the signal arm to danger. It was as late as 1893 before the railways agreed that red should signify danger, and green 'all clear'. Although many railways had already standardised these colours, some persisted with the use of purple for some signals to indicate danger, and white as 'all clear'.

When in the end the automatic continuous brake was adopted, the safety factor on British railways became something of which we could be, and still can be, proud.

CHAPTER 12

RAILWAYS AND RAILWAYMEN

In the world of commerce every corporate body can be divided into the shareholders who provide the capital; the employees who do the work and take something out of it; and finally the public, who form the customers, and therefore put in money to pay the wages and provide a dividend. The employees can be subdivided into two parts – the management who steer the company to provide greater efficiency and profits, thereby increasing their salaries; and the wage earning workers who are concerned mostly with the manual effort to supply the goods. This book would be incomplete unless some reference were made to the relationship between management and employees.

The attitude of the management was to keep a firm hand on the army of employees, and, indeed, no one will quarrel with the maintenance of discipline when public safety is at stake. The railways offered permanent employment to their men, and the specialised work and the security gave rise to a sense of vocation. Generation after generation served on the iron road so that you had 'railway families', who had railways in their blood, and the companies and the public benefited from the men's devotion and their pride in their own particular line.

From the start, the public enjoyed better protection than the employee; if their goods were lost or damaged in transit they were covered by the Carriers' Act of 1830, while in the case of personal injury they had rights at Common Law for compensation. But what of the railwayman? His work whether as driver, shunter or lengthman was dangerous and personal injury was frequent. In the event of accident he could rely only on his rights under Common Law which meant that he had to prove negligence by the company before receiving a penny. In 1837 his rights were further reduced by the text book case of Priestley v. Fowler which established that a workman was deemed to accept the risk of accident caused by the negligence of any one working for the same master, i.e. a fellow employee. With regard to discipline the strictness of the régime can be gauged from the case of John Hewitt, a driver on the Liverpool and Manchester Railway, who was dismissed on 10th February 1836 for being disgruntled and threatening to join a strike. He had no Union to rely upon. On the London & Birmingham Railway in 1838 a porter named John Brand was dismissed for accepting a 6d tip.

It is not surprising, therefore, to find that a modest society was founded in 1839 mainly for the purpose of providing some financial benefit for men injured at work or falling ill, and also to organise men into a fraternity which could deal better with managements. This was the Locomotive Steam Engine Drivers' and Firemen's Friendly Society. The society had plenty of work, for example it seemed desirable that engine drivers should receive more than 8s a day for their exacting and responsible work which extended over 80 hours each week. The Society would not interfere, however, when a gross breach of discipline occurred, and their membership was limited to drivers and firemen.

The year 1848 was unsettled in Europe, and the attempted revolutions in many countries adversely affected trade here. Managements tended to harden in their attitude during times of bad trade when profits were reduced and unemployment increased. Thus the period 1848–50 is one in which several strikes occurred and organised resistance from the men may be said to date from this time. The Locomotive Steam Engine Drivers' and Firemen's Friendly Society called out 240 men, but a strike of this size had little chance of success. But in 1853 business on the L.&N. W.R. was good, so that when porters at Liverpool asked for their wages to be increased from 18s to 19s a week, their request was granted. Station masters were considered comfortably off at £2 a week, and were men of importance in their localities.

However, among railway servants lapses did occur, as when a porter at Sharnbrook was drunk on duty. The *Bedfordshire Mercury* reports:

> '23rd August 1858. Sharnbrook. Committal of railway porter for being drunk.
>
> On Friday week, Heley Abbey, a porter on the Leicester & Hitchin Railway, stationed at Sharnbrook, was taken by Superintendent Graham before J. Gibbard Esq., on a charge of having been found drunk and incapable of performing his duty while in the employment of the Railway Company. Mr. J. Jeffrey, Inspector from Derby, attended on behalf of the Company to prefer the charge. Mr. T. Sheel, station master, proved the offence. The defendant admitted he was guilty and asked the magistrate to deal leniently with him. He was committed to gaol for seven days with hard labour.'

The company would have little difficulty in replacing the porter as they had long waiting lists.

In the matter of accidents, the law could appear unfair in its attitude to employees. In April 1865 a pick-up goods train had stopped at Southill on its way from Leicester to King's Cross. Thomas Charlton the guard informed William Oldham the driver that in the shunting they were to put off one wagon and pick up four. The first operation was carried out, but when Charlton went to hook on the four wagons he tripped and was crushed by the buffers. The inquest was held at *The White Horse* public house, and a verdict of accidental death was returned to Mr Whyley, the coroner. In November 1866 Thomas Adams, a lengthman, was walking towards Bedford along the 'four foot' on the down main line with his back to the trains, instead of following the normal practice of walking so that one faced the trains. Just as it was getting dusk he was run down and killed by an express. Again the verdict was accidental death. In both cases the dependants received not a penny. The law does not award damages in the case of a pure accident, that is to say, an accident not arising out of someone's negligence. But even if it could have been proved that the accident at Southill had been caused by Charlton tripping over material left near the track by a platelayer and that Adams was run down because the driver was not looking ahead, then the company would still have sheltered behind the doctrine of Common Employment. The employee was thus worse off than the fare paying public, as a passenger injured through the negligence of a railway servant would always be able to obtain compensation. It was not until 1880 that public opinion, acting through parliament and press, brought about the Employers' Liability Act (1880) which abolished the defence of Common Employment.

The 1860s therefore saw the men disunited and unable to bring pressure to bear on the managements to redress the main evils which beset their work: inadequate pay; excessive hours; and inherent danger. The footplatemen had a small society but support was weak, because many men had been nominated for employment by directors of the company and therefore considered themselves under an obligation. Others had had to deposit a sum of money as security, while yet others lived in companies' cottages at nominal rents. Some lines like the London Brighton & South Coast Railway gave an annual bonus of £5 to drivers and policemen. Furthermore, wages paid to engine crews compared favourably with those of other trades (1865) as follows: driver 45s a week; fireman 35s a week; farm labourer 11s 6d.

Excessive hours were commonplace. Investigation into an accident at Daubhill in January 1865 showed that a signalman had been working daily from 5.30 a.m. to 9 p.m., and in addition to his signalling duties had had to open and shut level crossing gates.

There was no danger for those on clerical work, but they too had long hours and low pay. On 11th October 1865 the second of the great unions was formed – the Railway Clerks' Association (now the Transport Salaried Staff's Association). The year 1867 was one of financial depression and it is not surprising to read of an outbreak of strikes, which on the whole were unsuccessful. In cases where the strikers won, the negotiations had taken place between themselves and the Directors, since the latter refused to recognise the unions. Where a strike collapsed, the unions lost members. The Locomotive Steam Engine Drivers' and Firemen's Society did not survive this year and was dissolved.

The Reform Act of 1867 meant that more railwaymen were entitled to vote, and more candidates were able to go to Parliament as railway members. The Railway Clerks' Association was becoming stronger, but could not assist the great mass of manual workers, who, since the end of the Locomotive Society had no unifying body, and had to rely on the protection afforded by the law. The inspectors of the Board of Trade, always vigilant for the safety of passengers, continued to deplore the excessive hours of work. In 1871 an increase in trade resulted in a demand for extra efforts by the railway workmen. Drivers were working $19\frac{1}{2}$ hours a day, and pointsmen 15 hours. Mr Bass, the M.P. for Burton on Trent, revealed in the Commons that a guard in 1870 had worked from 6.35 p.m. on 23rd December to 2 p.m. on 25th December without a break. At the same time a signalman had worked for $102\frac{1}{2}$ hours in a week. The men needed protection, and the Amalgamated Society of Railway Servants was formed in 1871 with W. Chapman as Secretary. Help came too from Gladstone with the Trade Union Act of 1871 which gave the society legal status, though strikes were still considered illegal. The first Great Delegate Meeting of the A.S.R.S. was held in London on 24th June 1872, and J. Abbott was the delegate from Bedford.

Board of Trade returns for 1872 showed that fifty-four railwaymen were killed while working, especially when shunting. The Board forced the Railway Companies to have destination tickets and brake levers on both sides of the wagons to save the shunters having to dodge between buffers to read the tickets or apply brakes. The membership of the A.S.R.S. was 17,247 in 1872 and this had fallen to 6,321 by 1882 largely because the provinces distrusted London. Nevertheless the Committee were able to open the Railway Orphanage at Derby in 1875. The next year Disraeli introduced a Trade Union Act which gave yet more strength to the Union movement.

The locomotive men had always considered themselves apart from the general railway workers, and claimed that their work required more skill and carried more responsibility. Previously they had had their own society, and in the last month of 1879 they created the Associated Society of Locomotive Engineers and Firemen, which is still active.

The last year of the decade saw the passing of the Employers' Liability

Act which abolished the doctrine of 'Common Employment', and there was now some redress when a man was injured or killed.

Bedford was chosen as a meeting place for the Associated Society of Railway Servants on 3rd April 1885, and the *Bedfordshire Mercury* reported:

'The Associated Society of Railway Servants held a meeting in Bedford on Good Friday 3rd April 1885 at Roff's Rooms, 34 High Street, Bedford, supported by Mr. Meredyth (Chief Constable) and presided over by Alderman Coombs. Mr. Ellis, Secretary of the A.S.R.S. was present. A band played music including the Caliph of Baghdad. The report for 1884 said that 214 orphans were in receipt of weekly payments costing £872 per annum. The proceedings ended with a toast of H.M. the Queen.'

In the same year Bedford was chosen by the Railway Temperance Union for their annual meeting, which was held in the Assembly Rooms on Wednesday 14th October 1885.

In 1889 came the Regulation of Railways Act which enforced the adoption of continuous automatic brakes, the block system of train control and the interlocking of points and signals. In the same year a split occurred in the Amalgamated Society of Railway Servants. At the A.G.M. the motion that lower grades of railway staff should contribute only 3d a week was defeated, and the disgruntled lower grades broke away and founded the General Railway Workers' Union.

As the century came to an end Parliament passed the first of the Workmen's Compensation Acts, and the Act of 1897 introduced the principle of compensation irrespective of negligence. Only certain trades were included, but railways were among them. Thus railway workers now had fair security, in addition to their pride in their job.

CHAPTER 13

CRIME

Not many people would have sympathised with Ruskin's denunciation of the railways, but even those who disliked them were happy to use the facilities the railways offered. Among the first eager customers were citizens both good and bad, and a petition to Quarter Sessions in 1860 from some leading Luton townsfolk asking for more police constables, shows how the railway there was used. The petitioners stated:

'That numerous attempts at Burglary and Housebreaking have been recently made at Luton some of which have succeeded and property to a considerable amount has been taken away and that very recently Two well known and experienced Thieves were apprehended in the Vestry Room of the Parish Church who made a desperate resistance but fortunately the Police were on the look out . . a complete set of Skeleton Keys and Housebreaking Implements were found in their possession . . That since the opening of the Railway from Luton to Hatfield, Thieves have much greater facility in disposing of their plunder by taking an early morning Train to London in little more than an hour and before the Police are aware of the Transaction . . .'

But trains were not just convenient for escaping, but also suitable for some sorts of theft. The modern corridor coach did not become common until the end of the 19th century, and the ordinary compartments were an ideal medium for the criminal, especially if they contained only one person. Thus the most common form of crime, during this period, was personal assault with robbery as the motive, for there was no communication between carriages.

Public opinion gave H. Sheridan the opportunity to introduce his Railways (Guards' and Passengers' Communication) Bill in May 1857, which though good in conception, did not go far enough. Railways could adopt any form of communication they wished, and the result was that many companies fitted unreliable systems to their coaches, which were in effect useless.

A murder by an immigrant called Muller in 1864 caused the greatest outcry, but the railways' response varied from gradually fitting Harrison's external cord, to fitting of 'Muller's lights' on the London & South

Western Railway. These were circular 'portholes' cut in the compartments so that what took place in one compartment could be heard in the whole carriage. Although there may have been an increase in safety, the holes met with mixed reception. The Harrison type of alarm had certain basic defects. For example, when attacked by a thief, the victim had to arrange a temporary truce while he let down the window, stood on the seat, and groped for a cord which ran outside the carriage. The cord could be imperfectly connected to the guard's van, and when the guard heard the bell he might choose to do nothing. Thieves, ignorant of the common courtesies of life, seldom complied.

Meanwhile annoyance and assault continued. As was often the case, it was the smaller southern railways who showed the most enterprise, while the large northern lines held aloof. In 1865, on the South Eastern Railway, many coaches were fitted with the Walker electric alarm system, and the London & South Western adopted the Preece system. Both were worked from batteries, and both gave the alarm by ringing a bell in the guard's van. Unfortunately, in practice, it was found that the contacts became corroded, and the alarm proved unreliable.

Railway crime was not, of course, confined to assault. There is a report in the *Bedfordshire Mercury* for 16th October 1865 of an attempted burglary at Leighton Buzzard station.

'Very early in the morning of Sunday 8th October 1865 a rough looking fellow was seen loitering about the station. Mr. Maltby, telegraph clerk, heard a crash and taking a light saw that someone had broken the window of the ticket office. He saw two men standing at the corner nearest the bridge crossing the line and called to them. They ran off. He went for assistance but they had decamped in the meantime. At the corner of the bridge were found a cudgel, a muffler, a whistle, a knife and a taper and matches.'

Fortunately on this occasion there was no loss and no one was hurt.

Meanwhile, the larger northern railways were beginning to show a belated interest in passenger-guard communication, and a meeting was arranged at Euston for Wednesday 17th January 1866 to see a demonstration of Howell's Patent Communication, a somewhat complicated device.

The *Bedfordshire Mercury* reports:

'Among those present were G. P. Neele, W. Cawkwell of the London & North Western Railway, J. Smithells of the London & York (Great Northern), Mr. Yoekney of the Sirhowy Railway and E. M. Needham of the Midland. *System*. A brass tube to run the length of the train with india rubber connections between cars, closed at one end, the other connected to the blast pipe of the engine, and so all the air is exhausted. A ball (numbered) is placed in an upright pipe in each compartment, covered by an airtight cap. By pulling a cord the cap opens and the rush of air sends the ball to the guard's van where it moves a trigger and explodes a detonator. The guard examines the ball and knows by the number from which compartment it came.

The rush of air also blows an external whistle to attract the attention of the driver. If the balls were hollow a message could be written and placed in. The experiment was completely successful.'

This ingenious arrangement would not have operated if the train stopped in a tunnel (a very likely place for an attack) as the engine would have no steam exhausting through the blast pipe. As for the message to be placed in a ball, the thief might show signs of impatience if the message were a long one.

The Great Western Railway was still content with the outside cord as late as 1874, when a bad accident at Shipton on Cherwell, on Christmas Eve, proved once more, if further proof were needed, that the outside cord was futile. It was now the turn of the Midland Railway to be the scene of a crime, unusual in some of its details.

Early in 1875 the Midland, always to the fore in the question of passenger comfort, had introduced Pullman coaches on some of its trains. These became immediately popular. Just before midnight on 14th June 1875 a young man named Harry Gustavus Hamilton took his seat in the Pullman coach attached to the train which departed punctually at 12 o'clock. He found his travelling companions genial, and their address was reassuring – they were the Reverend William Spragg, Herbert Willes, and Samuel Freeman. Soon after the train left St Pancras the three strangers suggested a game of cards, but when they found that they were unable to swindle Hamilton out of his money, they descended to assault and robbery. Hamilton put up a strong resistance, and had the coach been fitted with the modern alarm chain, he would have been able to put the guard on the alert and perhaps to have saved his life. As the train sped towards Flitwick he was thrust out of the carriage, and his body was found near the track next morning. Subsequently the three were arrested and charged with feloniously killing Harry Gustavus Hamilton. Herbert Willes had been too drunk to do much, but his companions received the maximum term of imprisonment. Spragg's clerical collar had been assumed merely to inspire confidence in his victims.

Although newspapers campaigned for better passenger communication, nothing much could be done until automatic continuous brakes were fitted to trains and this took place in the last decade of the century. With the Westinghouse system, pulling the alarm chain opened a valve in the train pipe and caused a slight application of the brake. The driver would feel a check to his speed, and the air pressure gauge on the locomotive would register a drop in pressure. The gauge in the guard's van would tell the same story. It was then for the driver to stop at once or proceed to the next station according to circumstances.

Once again, it was a small railway which led the way to safer travel. The Manchester Sheffield & Lincolnshire Railway (later the Great Central) evolved the modern system and it won immediate approval from the Board of Trade, and it was not long before every passenger train in this country, running on tracks of normal gauge, was suitably equipped.

CHAPTER 14

THE RAILWAY AGE – A SUMMARY

In 1838 when the first train on the London & Birmingham Railway passed through Rugby, Dr Arnold is reported as saying 'There goes the death-blow of feudality'. The editor of the *Railway Record* saw this clearly in July 1846 when he wrote in his leading article:

'Railways have effected a great social revolution. Brighton, the favoured retreat of Majesty . . . can now be reached by 2,000 passengers in a single train of 44 carriages, and at a cost of 5s return. The stage coach fare had been £1 and it took all day. The train left at 7 a.m. and arrived in Brighton at 9 a.m.'

After the Napoleonic wars, the country had entered a period of depression and unemployment combined with a rapidly rising population. The conditions in Bedfordshire are seen in the Woburn correspondence. There is a letter dated 15th September 1833 from Crocker, the Duke of Bedford's steward at Woburn, to W. G. Adam, Agent-in-chief in London:

' . . . there are so many unemployed in . . . Westoning, Flitton, Toddington, etc. and the feeling among them appears to reckless . . . There was a fire at Eaton Bray yesterday morning which destroyed the Tithe barn.'

In another letter (20th September 1834) Crocker mentions that farmers have lowered wages from 9s to 8s. Shortly afterwards, a new steward, Thomas Bennett states that 'at Steppingley . . the few farmers there are terrified out of their wits'. Well they might be, for Bennett reports that an outbuilding belonging to the Overseer of the Poor was set on fire, and glass broken in the houses of the Reverend Mr Green and Mr Cook. The burden of the losses by fire fell on to the insurance companies, and Bennett reports on 6th February 1835 that the County Fire Office have sent a police officer to Wilden to try and trace the incendiaries. Bennett saw before most people that the only permanent solution was mass emigration. in a letter to Adam written on 30th November 1834 he said ' . . . We have a surplus population . . . without some means . . . to dispose of this redundancy the Workhouse system will fail . . . If this is admitted we must turn . . . to emigration. [The demand for agricultural labour is only seasonal] and there is always plenty of Irish . . . The owners of the soil can never look to any permanent relief until a considerable part of the population will leave the Country altogether. We cannot expect to get many of the married people to go . . . and the single man is so much better off [on relief than a married man] that he will not look for anything better . . .'. The railways therefore played a part in ameliorating unemployment, though the large numbers of men needed when a line was being built were needed for too short a time. But any relief was welcomed. The *Bedfordshire Mercury* reported on 9th March 1863 that the Midland Railway was proposing to open a railway plant at Bedford capable of employing 1,000 persons. In fact this proposal came to nothing, but the railways did give steady employment to thousands of men throughout the last century.

The thirty years of comparative peace after Waterloo allowed an accretion of capital in Great Britain, and the growing railways system gave investors a use for their accumulated wealth. However, the capital could be used either for steady investment in sound railways, or in hasty speculation in unsound ones. The new industry made possible a new crime, and even the honest Buckinghamshire Railway was involved being the victim of scrip forgeries. Here is what the *Railway Record* said on 27th June 1846:

'Scrip Forgeries. The trial of Faulkner and Fabian on a charge of issuing forged scrip of the Buckinghamshire Railway has been postponed to the next sessions of the Central Criminal Court. The Recorder said "The enormous capital now invested in railways renders it necessary to take the greatest possible care to prevent fraud as much as possible".'

However, most railway stock was a very sound investment. A notebook kept by Francis Wythes of Ravensden House, near Bedford, shows a characteristic railway share list between 1846 and 1878. He had shares in 1878 in the Great Eastern Railway, London & North Western, Great Northern, North Staffordshire, London & South Western; Somerset & Dorset; and North Eastern Railway Company, lessees of the Whitby Redcar and Middlesboro' Union Railway Company.

The demand for land had tended towards inflationary prices, and both landowners and railway men accused the other side of unscrupulous behaviour. A letter from Thomas Bennett to Haedy of 4th January 1846 refers to the Bedford Railway and also to the Bedford and Cambridge Railway (1845). Mr Theed Pearse was the Bedford solicitor who worked for the Bedford line.

'I will communicate with Mr. Wing on the Bedfordshire Railways. As far as Bedfordshire is concerned, the lines in connexion with the

Birmingham & London, the Eastern Counties, and the Midland Counties, are those which are the most worthy of the Duke's support, but there may, on examination, be exceptions and some of the schemes may likewise not suit the Thorney Estate.

'I am sorry to find that Mr. Cuming and Mr. Sandars do not at all hit, and [are] not likely to agree. Mr. Pearse having lately bought land (subject to be flooded after every heavy rain) at £200 per acre, they are using this as a lever and are taking the high hand bullying tone, which appears to be Railway manners . . . I saw Mr. Pearse . . . and I said that Sandars had used his name as an authority for land being to be bought for £200 an acre close to Bedford, and I pointed out to him the difference of value in the estimation of practical builders between ground above reach of water, and that subject to be flooded and I also said that the bullying system would not go down with us and Mr. Sandars had now got our final offer. I further said that if the system was pursued, the Duke had not given assent to the Cambridge Extension and to the seven acres they meant to take from him for a station. They must therefore be prepared to encounter his Grace's opposition unless the price shall be agreed on beforehand. This appeared to alarm him, and he said he trusted the two would meet and agree and save any unpleasant proceedings between the Duke and the Company as the time is gone past for giving anyone else notice. I think we are safe in applying the screw. They must either buy the Duke's land or wait another year for their Act.'

In 1854 it is the Hitchin extension of the Midland which calls for a letter from Bennett and the following was written on 1st January:

'As the amount to which the land belonging to the Duke of Bedford is only some £1,500 or thereabouts, it cannot be of much avail, to the Directors, whether paid for at once or converted into shares, but I can easily imagine they may expect that the Duke's name along with other influential landowners on the line, will be of service to them, by such support.'

Bennett again refers to the Midland extension, and sighs for the happy days of 1846 when he writes to Haedy on 21st January 1855:

'No doubt the days for giving £1,000 an acre for Railway uses are past and gone – we must now be content with the pleasing reminiscence of those sunny times.

'The Hitchin and Leicester take about 1½ acre on the south of Elstow Road, which I sold some months ago at three hundred pounds an acre . . .'

Sunday travel caused trouble, and the Church of England found itself in alliance with sects with whom it normally had little in common, over this vexed question. Excursions were the main target. Sir John Easthope, Chairman of the London & South Western Railway, was not a man to be easily intimidated. Archdeacon Hoare of Winchester perceived with the most unfeigned regret that the day of religious rest was constantly dese-crated by the running of trains upon the railway and suggested that the Divine blessing could scarcely be expected to rest upon the South Western Railway in consequence. Sir John Easthope rebutted the statement, and imputed that the Diocesan authorities were concerned only with pre-venting the movement of common people on the day when labour did not keep them in their place. This was in 1846.

The London & North Western Railway was one of the few to dis-courage Sunday excursion trains. This rule was enforced while Captain Huish was General Manager. The *Bedfordshire Mercury* quotes his remarks in 1862:

'Sunday Railway Work
Captain Huish, for 18 years Chief Manager of the London & North Western Railway bears the following business testimony on the subject:

"In answer to your enquiry and your desire to have my opinion in regard to Sunday excursion trains, gathered from my 18 years' experience as General Manager of the L.N.W.R., I can only say that during that time no excursion trains ever ran on a Sunday; and I am satisfied that while the interests of the proprietors did not suffer, the discipline and character of the Company were promoted.

"I have had a large experience of excursion traffic and was always favourable to its development, but I believe no Company ultimately benefits by working its system to the extent of seven days a week, and that by a well arranged system of Saturday trains returning on a Monday an equal pecuniary return at a much less cost is produced. Putting the question therefore on the lowest ground of argument, I have no hesitation in saying that a railway Company consults its true interests in restraining Sunday work within as *narrow* limits as pos-sible. The Scotch railways as a whole pay better than the English ones and there the work on a Sunday is reduced to a minimum.'

The Captain, writing from his Isle of Wight home after retirement, puts the case well, but he overlooks the fact that many people want a one day excursion and not three, as he suggests, particularly if you take into account the additional cost of two nights' lodging. From the railways' point of view, Sunday excursions have the merit of occupying tracks which are free from the more crowded weekday services. If it were true that Scottish railways were more profitable than English ones, it does not follow that the reason is the banning of Sunday excursion trains.

More opposition came from hunting people, who were afraid that the railway would interfere with their activities. When the Midland line from Leicester to Hitchin was being built, there were protests from the Shires, and in his letter to Haedy of 1st January 1854 Thomas Bennett is probably referring to the Oakley Hunt.

'I believe many of the Hunting people think the Rail will be injurious to their sport; whether it will, or no, may be known from the experience of other hunting districts through which Railways pass, but this cannot much signify, from the low ebb to which fox-hunting has come in Bedfordshire . . . But there can be no doubt that any line going through a district, must eventually, indirectly or directly, tend to its improved value.'

The railways brought a new threat to the welfare of farm animals because of the speed with which livestock could be moved from place to place. The cattle plague, or foot and mouth disease, had always been a scourge, but it could be confined within known geographical limits up to, say, 1850. But now animals could be on a farm in Kent one day, and be detrained in Cumberland on the next, and disease was spread quickly over the countryside. Also, despite some hesitation to begin with, the railway companies had begun to develop a traffic in truckloads of stable manure, and this also could carry infection. There was a virulent outbreak of cattle plague in the years 1865–66, and the Bedfordshire Quarter Sessions minutes reflect local concern. At the adjourned Epiphany Session on 19th January 1866 the Clerk of the Peace read a copy of the following letter sent by the Clerk to the Toseland Justices to the Home Secretary.

'Saint Neots
Sir,   18th January 1866
Cattle Plague
I am directed by the Justices of the Peace for the Toseland Division of the County of Huntingdon to inform you that in the Petty Sessional Division of Toseland and to a much greater extent in the adjoining County of Bedford many acres are annually sown with Onion seed in the month of February – for this crop a large quantity of manure is used which is not ploughed in but is spread upon the surface and is sometimes harrowed in but often only raked over so as to make a level surface and the greater part of the manure remains on the surface.

The Justices are informed that the gardeners in this neighbourhood are bringing down large quantities of manure from London by the

Great Northern Railway to the Saint Neots Station which will be used for the Onion crop as above stated and they think that there can be no doubt that much of this Manure will come from cow sheds where animals have been kept which have died of the cattle plague and that there is great danger of the plague being extensively spread by means of this manure.

The Justices are informed that in several instances parts of animals (supposed to have died of the plague) have been sent down in the manure trucks.'

As a result, the Chairman of the Bedfordshire Quarter Sessions had an interview with managers of the Midland and of the Great Northern Railways, and gave his report on 3rd February:

'The Great Northern send nothing but horse manure from King's Cross so far as they are aware.

'The Midland Company the same.

'The Great Northern employ a man to inspect the loading of manure to see that it does not contain any portion of carcases.

'The Midland Company's representative undertook to do the same.

'The Great Northern suggested a form of Certificate to be handed to them by the senders of manure which they and the Midland agreed to adopt provided the Metropolitan authorities agreed to give their Inspectors instructions to sign them.

'Failing this Certificate the Great Northern and Midland expressed their willingness to refuse manure which they suspected as coming from infected stables or places.

'RESOLVED . . . that unless the London and North Western Railway Company consent to the same conditions as have been agreed to on behalf of the Great Northern and Midland Railways the Court may be compelled to prohibit the conveyance of manure etc. into this county by the London and North Western Railway.

'RESOLVED that whereas . . . the Justices of Bedfordshire have agreed with the Directors of the G.N.R. and Midland Railway that no manure shall be sent into that county by the said companies unless the sender produce to the agent of the said company a certificate signed by an Inspector of Police of the District from which the manure is brought stating that to the best of his belief such manure does not come from any infected premises.

'The said Justices do hereby request that Sir Richard Mayne will give orders to the Inspectors of the Metropolitan Police to sign such certificates when they can with truth do so . . .

'that the said Justices . . . have resolved and determined to declare and do hereby declare

'That it is expedient that until the 1st day of March next ensuing no raw or untanned hide, skin, hoof or offal . . . shall be brought from any place in Great Britain into the county of Bedford . . .

'That it is expedient that until the 1st day of March next ensuing no dung, hay, straw, fodder or litter likely to propagate infection shall be removed from any place in the said county where the cattle plague exists . . or has existed within a period of 42 days next previously thereto, to any other place within the said county,

'That it is expedient that until the 1st day of March next ensuing no sheep, lamb, goat, or swine shall be removed from any part of the county of Bedford where the cattle plague exists at the time of such intended removal or has existed within a period of 42 days next previously thereto, to any other place within the said county . . .'

The outbreak lasted until late in the year, for on 31st July 1866 proceedings were taken against a farmer and a railway goods clerk who had apparently collaborated to defeat the law. It appears that the L.N.W.R. had removed some cattle, seven cows and a calf, from Winslow in Buckinghamshire to Leighton Buzzard without a magistrate's licence. A licence had been obtained to move the beasts from Winslow to Granborough, two miles away, but Bailey, the farmer, wanted to get his beasts to Leighton market, so he told the goods clerk at Winslow that the word 'Granborough' was a clerical error, and should be altered to 'Leighton'. The clerk did so, without troubling to verify the statement, and both were fined the sum of 2s 6d.

The very nature of a railway company's business, that is, the carriage of goods and passengers at high speeds for long distances, and the use of machines which could emit sparks, soon meant that they were hedged in with legal liabilities. The type of locomotive used made the emission of sparks an everyday occurrence, and claims for compensation were pressed home by owners of property damaged by fire. At Kempston Hardwick, on 2nd August 1858, the 4 a.m. train from Bedford set fire to some growing corn, consisting of 10 acres of barley belonging to John Emery and 5½ acres of wheat the property of Robert Whitworth, on the other side of the line. The fire hazard was particularly great in August when the corn was dry and ripe and ready for harvesting. The *Bedfordshire Mercury* reported an incident at Sandy on 4th May 1863:

'A serious fire occurred at Warren Farm, the property of Arthur Peel Esq., in the occupation of Mr. Robertson, on Monday 27th April, between 9 and 10 a.m. The fire was caused by a spark thrown from an engine of the Bedford & Cambridge Railway. The Sandy,

Potton and Biggleswade engines were quickly on the spot, but nearly the entire newly erected farm buildings were destroyed, and a large quantity of potatoes and some farm implements. The total damage is £800.'

An attempt to obtain money for lack of reasonable care was disclosed in a case against the L.&N.W. Railway heard at the Luton County Court in 1859. Mrs Oliver was the owner of a Turin vase and some wax flowers which she was taking from Liverpool to Luton. She changed trains at Leighton Buzzard. She said that she examined the vase and flowers on arrival at Luton station and found them damaged. She stated that she had carried the parcel on her lap from Liverpool to Leighton, but she entrusted the parcel to the guard when she entered the local train at Leighton Buzzard. Unfortunately for her, she made contradictory statements under cross-examination, changing her story to having placed the parcel in the care of the guard at Liverpool. Mr Justice Coe was not impressed and found for the defendants. On hearing that his wife had lost her case, Mr Oliver, in a fury, stated that the judge had called him a liar, and that he kept company with better people than the judge. He then left the court 'in a dreadful rage'.

The increasing liabilities placed upon the public gave insurance companies their chance and they soon had schemes for policies of every description – Personal Accident in case of a train smash; Life Assurance so that dependants would be protected; Baggage and Parcel Insurance to cover loss and damage. The first company to embark on accident insurance was the Railway Passengers' Assurance Company, which commenced business in 1849. The following letter, an advertisement in the *Railway Times*, shows the benefit of insurance cover:

'Dunstable,
28th November 1849

I was travelling by railway from Penrith to Preston on the night of the 1st inst., and having occasion to go out of the train at the latter station, by the carelessness of the porter I was led over the edge of the turntable and seriously injured on the head and ribs, and three of my teeth force out, which laid me up for several days. I had previously effected an insurance against railway accidents, with the Railway Passengers Assurance Company, and when sufficiently able to get up to London, I at once gave notice to the officers of that Company, in Old Broad Street, that I had met with an accident. They immediately sent their medical officer to Mullins Hotel where I was staying, and in the course of a few days I was well enough to make my claim in person at the offices of the above Company.

I adduced evidence of my costs, both for medical attendance in the country and in London, and my hotel expenses, and within three weeks after the day of the accident received the compensation which I thought fit to demand, without demur or the loss of an hour's time.

William Good'

The railways naturally did what they could to avoid losing money. One way was the public's desire to travel without payment, which is no new thing. One William Pepper was convicted in Bedford in 1858 of travelling in a Midland train to Shefford with intent to avoid paying the fare. He was convicted, but the conviction was quashed on appeal. The railway companies have always been worried by the amount they have to pay for the occupation of land and buildings, particularly as in more recent years, some of the money which they have paid has gone to improve the roads, their great competitors. The L.&N.W. Railway appealed on 19th October 1870 against the rates levied on property at Kempston and Goldington. The appeal was 'respited' no fewer than eight times, and finally on 1st January 1873 was dismissed for both places. The company had better fortune in 1878 when an appeal was lodged on 10th April in respect of railway buildings in Lidlington, Marston, Willington, Cople, Cardington, Eastcotts, Wootton, Kempston and Elstow. It was respited until 4th June of the same year, when the railway managed to obtain reductions for six of the stations.

When the first railways opened, each station used its local time, and when the line was short, or ran from north to south, there was no confusion. But railways like the Great Western and also the London & North Western extended across several lines of longitude, and Plymouth time, for example, was about 20 minutes after Paddington time. The Board of Trade inspectors were the first to complain and to ask for uniform time. So when the L.&N.W. opened their Trent Valley line (Rugby to Stafford) in 1847, they compelled all the stations to use London time and this applied to all L.N.W.R. stations. Other lines followed suit in due course.

Advertising spread to station platforms, although the newspapers still held first place. The *Bedfordshire Mercury* in 1847 had the following:

'Joseph Manning of Threadneedle Street, London, who supplied the drink for the opening of the Bedford Railway, offers Champagne 54s a dozen, Single Stout 4s 6d a dozen.'

A more usual advertisement in this paper was:

'COALS! COALS!! COALS!!!

The best and cheapest coal supplied by Joseph Firbank, address: Head Office, North Western Station, Bedford.'

Not only did the railways themselves stand high in public esteem, but railway officials enjoyed considerable social standing. The station master of 100 years ago wore a frock coat and a top hat, and was well-known in his town, for he would make it his business to call on everyone who could provide custom for the railway. He was a person who would be asked for references. Therefore when Mr John Robinson was about to leave Sandy (L.N.W.) for Rugeley, a well-deserved promotion, he was presented with a silver cup with the inscription:

'Presented by the inhabitants of Sandy to John Robinson as a mark of their high estimation of his merits and general attention as station master of the London & North Western Railway station at Sandy from August 1862 to February 1867.'

The staff of a large station was much more numerous in the 19th century and from such large numbers it was easy to pick a cricket eleven. Friendly matches were arranged, such as that between Kempston and the Midland Railway, Bedford, on 4th September 1869. The Midland team won by an innings, and had two excellent bowlers in King and Stanley.

What did the railways do for Bedfordshire? Very much what they did for the country as a whole. People were given the benefit of fast, cheap and safe travel, and so the travel habit was started which has never stopped. People now know more about their own country. Employment was given to thousands when the railways were built, and to thousands more who ran them. Bedford became the hub of a wheel with six spokes radiating from it, and so was easily in touch with all the neighbouring towns. Luton would not have developed its industry without the railway, and until 1948 there was no town in England more than 10 miles from a station. Against these advantages there was the smoke nuisance near engine sheds, noise of shunting in sidings, and the depreciation of property near railways. But when once the embankments and cuttings have grassed over, it is often difficult to see where a line crosses the countryside, and as a train carries people in the mass, there are fewer trains. In contrast, the motorways bring a roar of vehicles that does not cease day and night.

Despite press criticism, our railways today (in the field of technical efficiency) were never better. Speeds reach 100 m.p.h. daily with the latest electronic equipment at the lineside and in signal boxes. Foreign railway executives, who are the best people to judge, marvel at the density of our traffic, and the speed allied with punctuality. Turbine driven trains (tried here in 1959 but found unreliable) in an improved version will be able to run at 125 m.p.h. in a few years. The aeroplane has to lift everything before it can transport it, so heavy traffic is ruled out, and although road traffic carries many passengers and much of the most profitable freight, it does so at a frightening cost in human life and limb. One of the strange facets of 20th century society is that the sacrifice is tolerated. As an American writer has said 'People are no longer interested in safety'. Although many branch lines have been cut off, because the last four Transport Acts have insisted on the railways balancing their budget, and the total route mileage has dropped from 19,000 to 13,000, what is left is the cream of the system, and it is encouraging to find that receipts from the all important freight traffic increase each year. We can therefore regard the railways' future with sober confidence.

Appendix A

Timetables for L.N.W.R. and branches

A.1 *November 1846 Bedford Railway* (worked by L. & N.W.R.)

Euston	dep.	7.15 a.m.	10.45	4.00 p.m.	5.30
Bedford	arr.	10.15	1.15 p.m.	6.30	8.00
Bedford	dep.	7.15 a.m.	10.00	2.10 p.m.	5.50
Euston	arr.	10.20	12.30 p.m.	5.00	8.15

A.2 *June 1848 Bedford Railway* (worked by L. & N.W.R.)

		Weekdays					Sundays	
Bedford	dep.	7.05	9.45	11.45	2.05	5.55	8.20	3.00
Marston	arr.	7.18	9.58	12.00	2.20	6.10	8.35	3.15
Lidlington	,,	7.19	—	12.01	2.21	6.11	8.36	3.16
Ridgmount	,,	7.21	—	12.03	2.23	6.13	8.38	3.18
Woburn Sands	,,	7.36	10.13	12.20	2.40	6.30	8.55	3.35
Fenny Stratford	,,	7.44	—	12.28	2.48	6.38	9.03	3.43
Bletchley	,,	7.51	10.26	12.35	2.55	6.45	9.10	3.50
London	,,	10.10	12.00	3.00	5.00	8.30	—	6.00
London	dep.	7.15	11.00	12.30	3.45	5.30	7.30	—
Bletchley	arr.	9.08	12.47	2.20	5.20	7.12	9.08	4.00
Fenny Stratford	,,	9.35	1.20	3.20	—	7.20	9.35	4.08
Woburn Sands	,,	9.45	1.30	3.30	5.33	7.30	9.45	4.18
Ridgmount	,,	9.51	1.36	3.36	—	7.36	9.51	4.24
Lidlington	,,	9.53	1.38	3.38	—	7.38	9.53	4.26
Marston	,,	10.03	1.48	3.48	5.48	7.48	10.03	4.36
Bedford	,,	10.15	2.00	4.00	6.00	8.00	10.15	4.48

A.3 *September 1860 London & North Western Railway*

		Weekdays				Sundays
Bedford	dep.	7.15	9.50	4.10	6.50	7.27
Ampthill*	arr.	7.26	10.01	4.20	7.00	7.37
Lidlington	,,	7.32	—	4.26	7.06	7.47
Ridgmount	,,	7.39	—	4.32	7.13	7.55
Woburn Sands	,,	7.45	10.15	4.38	7.20	
Fenny Stratford	,,	7.53	—	—	7.28	8.05
Bletchley	,,	7.58	10.25	4.48	7.33	8.10
Leighton Buzzard	,,	8.19	10.46	5.18	9.07	8.27
Euston	,,	10.05	12.00	6.35	9.30	10.20
Northampton	,,	9.10	11.30	6.20	8.35	10.35
Oxford	,,	9.50	12.50	6.30	10.10	12.55
Rugby	,,	9.50	11.35	6.50	9.12	11.06
Birmingham	,,	11.10	12.25	8.15	10.25	12.30

[*Name of station changed to Ampthill (Marston).]

A.4   *July 1890* *London & North Western Railway*

						Weekdays						*Sundays*	
			a.m.									a.m.	p.m.
Cambridge	dep.		7.50	11.25		1.48			4.40	7.00		8.45	6.50
Lords Bridge	,,		8.00	—		1.57			4.50	7.12		8.57	—
Old North Road	,,		8.10	11.43		2.06			5.00	7.23		9.08	—
Gamlingay	,,		8.18	11.54		2.14			5.09	7.33		9.18	7.15
Potton	,,		8.24	12.01		2.21			5.15	7.38		9.23	7.22
Sandy	,,		8.32	12.10	12.25	2.27			5.23	7.47		9.32	7.33
Blunham	,,		8.38	12.17	12.31	2.33			5.29	7.53		9.38	7.40
Bedford	,,	7.30	8.51	12.31	12.42	2.47	5.15	5.41		8.05		9.55	7.54
Millbrook	,,	7.41	9.02	12.41	—	2.58	5.26	—		8.16		10.06	8.05
Lidlington	,,	7.46	9.07	—		3.05	5.31	—		8.21		10.11	—
Ridgmount	,,	7.53	9.14	—		3.13	5.38	—		8.28		10.18	—
Woburn Sands	,,	8.00	9.21	12.57		3.20	5.45	—		8.35		10.25	8.18
Fenny Stratford	,,	8.07	9.28	—		3.26	5.52	—		8.41		10.31	—
Bletchley	arr.	8.10	9.31	1.05		3.30	5.55	6.03		8.45		10.35	8.25

						Weekdays							
Bletchley	dep.	8.25 a.m.	9.05			11.40	1.40	2.10	4.10	6.25	9.25
Fenny Stratford	,,	8.27	—			—	1.43	—	4.13	6.28	9.28
Woburn Sands	,,	8.33	9.12			11.47	1.49	—	4.20	6.35	9.35
Ridgmount	,,	8.39	—			11.52	1.57	—	4.27	6.42	9.42
Lidlington	,,	8.44	—			—	2.03	—	4.33	6.48	9.49
Millbrook	,,	8.48	—			—	2.07	—	4.39	6.54	9.54
Bedford	,,	9.00	9.34	11.50	12.07	2.18	2.45	4.52	7.08	10.05
Blunham	,,	9.11	9.44	12.01	12.17	——	2.55	5.04	7.20	——
Sandy Junc.	,,	9.16	9.49	12.09	12.23		3.00	5.16	7.26
Potton	,,		9.55	——	12.32		3.08	5.26	7.37
Gamlingay	,,		10.00		12.38		3.15	5.34	7.45
Old North Road	,,		10.10		12.48		3.26	5.45	7.56
Lords Bridge	,,		10.20		12.58		3.37	5.56	8.07
Cambridge	arr.		10.30		1.10		3.49	6.10	8.19

		Sundays
Bletchley	dep.	11.35 a.m.
Fenny Stratford	,,	—
Woburn Sands	,,	11.42
Ridgmount	,,	11.49
Lidlington	,,	11.56
Millbrook	,,	12.01
Bedford	,,	12.14
Blunham	,,	12.26
Sandy Junction	,,	12.32
Potton	,,	12.43
Gamlingay	,,	12.51
Old North Road	,,	1.02
Lords Bridge	,,	1.13
Cambridge	,,	1.25

[Note: trains between Sandy Junction and Bedford only; Willington station was not opened until 1903 for passengers.]

A.5   *July 1850   London & North Western Railway*

Weekdays only

Euston Square	dep.	9.00 a.m. (Express)	5.30 p.m. (1st & 2nd only)
Leighton Buzzard	arr.	10.00	7.00
Dunstable	arr.	10.45	7.45

Bletchley	dep.	9.35 a.m. (1st & 2nd only)	6.50 p.m. (1st & 2nd only)
Leighton Buzzard	arr.	9.50	7.05
Dunstable	arr.	10.45	7.45

A.6   *July 1890   London & North Western Railway*

Weekdays only

Euston	dep.	6.00	8.00	9.30	10.15	11.45	3.15	6.00	7.10
Leighton Buzzard	,,	7.57	9.30	10.27	12.20	2.45	4.45	7.15	9.35
Stanbridgeford	,,	8.06	Sig.	10.37	Sig.	Sig.	Sig.	Sig.	Sig.
Dunstable	arr.	8.12	9.45	10.44	12.35	3.00	5.00	7.30	9.50

Dunstable	dep.	7.25	9.00	10.05	11.23	1.28	3.05	6.05	8.20
Standbridgeford	,,	7.32	9.05	10.10	11.30	1.34	3.10	6.12	8.27
Leighton Buzzard	arr.	7.42	9.15	10.20	11.40	1.43	3.20	6.22	8.37
Euston	,,	9.35	10.25	—	1.55	4.10	5.25	7.35	11.15

[As regards Down Trains the word 'Sig' means that the train stops only to set down passengers if prior notice is given to the guard, and to pick up passengers provided a clear signal is given to the engine driver.]

Appendix B

Timetables for M.R. and branches

B.1   *May 1857   Midland Railway*

		Weekdays				Sundays	
Leicester	dep.	6.00	8.00	1.00	5.35	—	—
Bedford	dep.	8.15	10.36	3.15	8.06	10.06 a.m.	8.06 p.m.
Cardington	arr.	—	10.46	—	8.16	10.16	8.16
Southill	,,	—	10.58	—	8.28	10.28	8.28
Shefford	,,	8.30	11.06	3.40	8.35	10.36	8.36
Henlow	,,	—	11.15	—	8.45	10.45	8.45
Hitchin	,,	9.00	11.30	4.00	9.00	11.00	9.00
King's Cross	arr.	10.15	12.45	5.05	10.25	—	—

King's Cross	dep.	—	6.30	10.00	5.00	—	—
Hitchin	,,	6.00	8.15	11.00	6.00	7.30	5.30
Henlow	arr.	—	8.27	—	6.12	7.42	5.42
Shefford	,,	6.19	8.35	11.19	6.20	7.50	5.50
Southill	,,	—	8.43	11.27	6.28	7.58	5.58
Cardington	,,	—	8.55	—	6.40	8.10	6.10
Bedford	,,	6.42	9.05	11.47	6.50	8.20	6.20
Leicester	,,	9.00	11.45	2.05	9.36	—	—

[Note the poor service at Henlow and Cardington.]

B.2   *September 1860.   Midland Railway*

		Weekdays					Sundays	
Class		1 & 2	1, 2 & 3	1 & 2	1, 2 & 3	1 & 2	1, 2 & 3	1, 2 & 3
Leeds	dep.	3.00	—	8.30	12.30	4.25	—	7.00
Sheffield	,,	4.05	—	9.35	1.10	5.15	—	8.15
Derby	,,	6.00	8.10	11.50	2.25	6.40	—	11.30
Nottingham	,,	6.00	8.05	11.45	2.30	6.35	—	11.30
Burton	,,	—	7.55	11.25	1.45	5.40	—	—
Leicester	,,	7.10	9.35	12.55	4.00	7.45	7.30	5.30 p.m.
Market Harborough	,,	7.38	10.19	1.27	4.44	8.11	8.19	6.19
Kettering	,,	7.55	10.48	1.44	5.13	8.20	8.52	6.52
Wellingborough	,,	8.08	11.10	1.56	5.35	8.43	9.16	7.16
Irchester	,,	*	11.17	—	5.42	—	9.24	7.25
Northampton	,,	—	9.20	11.30	4.30	7.05	—	10.35
Peterborough	,,	—	9.00	11.40	3.40	5.45	—	12.45
Sharnbrook	,,	8.26	11.32	2.11	5.57	—	9.41	7.41
Oakley	,,	—	11.42	—	6.06	—	9.53	7.53
Bedford	,,	8.40	11.55	2.25	6.18	9.08	10.06	8.06
Cardington	,,	*	12.03	—	6.25	—	10.16	8.16
Southill	,,	8.53	12.17	—	6.38	—	10.28	8.28
Shefford	,,	8.58	12.24	2.42	6.44	—	10.36	8.36
Hitchin	,,	9.15	12.50	3.05	7.10	9.35	11.05	9.05
Cambridge	,,	10.55	—	4.30	9.00	—	9.05 p.m.	—
King's Cross	arr.	10.05	1.35	3.50	8.00	10.20	11.50	9.50

*Stops to take up only.
[The above timetable appeared as an advertisement in the *Bedfordshire Mercury* for 1st September 1860.
The railway is referred to as 'The Midland Counties Railway' although this title was dropped in 1844.]

B.3   *July 1867   Midland Railway*

Class		*1 & 2*	*1, 2 & 3*	*1 & 2*	*1 & 2*	*1 & 2*	*1 & 2*	*1 & 2*	*,1 2 & 3*
					Weekdays				
King's Cross	dep.	6.25 a.m.	7.20	9.10	11.00	11.30	3.00 p.m.	3.40	5.35
Hitchin	,,	—	8.18	—	11.45	—	—	4.27	—
Henlow	,,	—	8.28	—	—	—	—	4.38	—
Shefford	,,	—	8.35	—	11.57	—	—	4.45	—
Southill	,,	—	8.42	—	12.03	—	—	4.51	—
Cardington	,,	—	8.51	—	—	—	—	5.02	—
Bedford	,,	7.32	9.00	10.13	12.18	12.40	4.08	5.09	6.41
Oakley	,,	—	9.08	—	—	—	—	5.20	—
Sharnbrook	,,	7.45	9.19	—	12.31	—	—	5.30	—
Northampton	arr.	8.40	10.15	11.50	—	1.40	5.05	6.40	7.40
Irchester	dep.	—	9.33	—	—	—	—	5.45	—
Wellingborough	,,	8.01	9.39	10.40	12.45	1.05	4.33	5.52	E
Kettering	,,	8.13	9.59	10.55	12.57	—	4.45	6.14	—
Market Harborough	,	8.33	10.26	——	1.16	—	5.03	6.39	E
Leicester	,,	9.00	11.10		1.45	1.55	5.28	7.30	7.50
Burton on Trent	arr.	10.40	1.30 p.m.		—	4.15	—		9.25
Nottingham	,,	10.25	12.55		3.10	—	6.30	—	8.40
Derby	,,	10.20	1.15		3.15	—	6.30	—	8.50
Sheffield	,,	11.55	3.35		4.25	—	8.10	—	10.00
Leeds	,,	12.30	5.05		5.15	—	9.35	—	10.45

Class		Weekdays		Sundays		
		1 & 2	*1 & 2*	*1, 2 & 3*	*1, 2 & 3*	*1 & 2*
King's Cross	dep.	6.30 p.m.	8.48	6.45 a.m.	5.55 p.m.	8.48
Hitchin	,,	7.23	—	7.33	6.43	—
Henlow	,,	A	—	7.47	6.55	—
Shefford	,,	7.35	—	7.54	7.01	—
Southill	,,	7.41	—	8.00	7.07	—
Cardington	,,	7.49	—	8.12	7.18	—
Bedford	,,	7.57	9.53	8.22	7.27	9.53
Oakley	,,	—	—	8.36	7.38	—
Sharnbrook	,,	8.12	—	8.45	7.49	—
Northampton	arr.	9.25	—	10.20	8.40	—
Irchester	dep.	8.24	—	9.01	8.03	—
Wellingborough	,,	8.32	10.17	9.08	8.09	10.17
Kettering	,,	8.48	10.29	9.28	8.28	10.29
Market Harborough	,,	9.09	10.45	9.59	—	10.45
Leicester	,,	9.45	11.10	10.50	—	11.10
Burton on Trent	arr.	—	12.53 p.m.	7.35 p.m.	—	12.53 a.m.
Nottingham	,,	12.15	12.15	6.10	—	12.15
Derby	,,	12.18	—	8.15	—	12.18
Sheffield	,,	2.10 a.m.	—	5.35	—	2.10
Leeds	,,	3.00	—	6.55	—	3.00

Note: A or E stops to set down only.

B.4 *July 1868 Midland Railway*

		Weekdays						Sundays	
Bedford	dep.	—	8.45	12.12	3.07	5.35	7.05	8.14	7.30 p.m.
Ampthill	,,	—	9.01	12.28	3.23	5.51	7.21	8.30	7.46
Harlington	,,	—	9.12	12.39	3.34	6.02	7.32	8.41	7.57
Leagrave	,,	—	9.24	12.51	3.46	6.14	7.44	8.53	8.09
Luton	,,	8.05	9.33	1.00	3.55	6.23	7.53	9.02	8.18
Chiltern Green	,,	8.12	9.41	1.08	—	6.31	8.01	9.10	8.26
Harpenden	,,	8.18	9.48	1.15	4.06	6.38	8.08	9.17	8.33
St Albans	,,	8.28	10.00	1.27	4.18	6.50	8.20	9.29	8.45
Radlett	,,	8.37	10.11	1.38	—	7.01	8.31	9.40	8.56
Elstree	,,	8.44	10.19	1.46	4.33	7.09	8.39	9.48	9.04
Mill Hill	,,	8.52	10.27	1.54	—	7.17	8.47	9.56	9.12
Hendon	,,	8.58	10.33	2.00	4.44	7.23	8.53	10.02	9.18
Finchley Road	,,	—	10.41	2.08	4.52	7.31	9.01	10.10	9.26
Haverstock Hill	,,	—	10.45	2.12	4.56	7.35	9.05	10.14	9.30
Kentish Town	,,	—	10.50	2.17	5.01	7.40	9.10	10.19	9.35
Camden Road	,,	—	10.53	2.20	5.04	7.43	9.13	10.22	9.38
King's Cross	,,	9.15	10.57	2.24	5.08	7.47	9.17	10.26	9.42
Farringdon St	,,	9.19	11.01	2.28	5.12	7.51	9.21	10.30	9.46
Aldersgate St	,,	9.21	11.03	2.30	5.14	7.53	9.23	10.32	9.48
Moorgate St	arr.	9.23	11.05	2.32	5.16	7.55	9.25	10.34	9.50

Note: The main line through trains will continue to run to and from the Great Northern station at King's Cross until further notice.

[Trains on this timetable refer only to stations between Bedford and Moorgate Street.]

Moorgate St	dep.	—	9.10	1.22	4.16	5.10	7.10	8.33	8.05	7.00
Aldersgate St	,,	—	9.12	1.24	4.18	5.12	7.12	8.35	8.07	7.02
Farringdon St	,,	—	9.14	1.26	4.20	5.14	7.14	8.37	8.09	7.04
King's Cross	,,	—	9.18	1.30	4.24	5.18	7.18	8.41	8.13	7.08
Camden Road	,,	—	9.22	1.34	4.28	5.22	7.22	8.45	8.17	7.12
Kentish Town	,,	—	9.25	1.37	4.31	5.25	7.25	8.48	8.20	7.15
Haverstock Hill	,,	—	9.31	1.43	4.37	5.31	7.31	8.54	8.26	7.21
Finchley Road	,,	—	9.35	1.47	4.41	5.35	7.35	8.58	8.30	7.25
Hendon	,,	—	9.43	1.55	4.49	5.43	7.43	9.06	8.38	7.33
Mill Hill	,,	—	9.50	2.02	—	5.50	7.50	9.13	8.45	7.40
Elstree	,,	—	9.58	2.10	5.00	5.58	7.58	9.21	8.53	7.48
Radlett	,,	—	10.05	2.17	—	6.05	8.05	9.28	9.00	7.55
St Albans	,,	—	10.17	2.29	5.15	6.17	8.17	9.40	9.12	8.07
Harpenden	,,	—	10.27	2.39	5.25	6.27	8.27	9.50	9.22	8.17
Chiltern Green	,,	—	10.34	2.46	—	6.34	8.34	9.57	9.29	8.24
Luton	,,	7.35	10.44	2.56	5.39	6.44	8.44	10.07	9.39	8.34
Leagrave	,,	7.44	10.54	3.06	5.49	—	8.54	—	9.49	8.44
Harlington	,,	7.53	11.03	3.15	5.58	—	9.03	—	9.58	8.53
Ampthill	,,	8.04	11.14	3.26	6.09	—	9.14	—	10.09	9.04
Bedford	arr.	8.20	11.30	3.42	6.25	—	9.30	—	10.25	9.20

[Notice that Cricklewood, West Hampstead and Flitwick stations are missing. Flitwick was opened in 1870.]

B.5   *July 1890   Midland Railway*

Weekdays

		5.15 a.m.	6.10	7.55	9.05	10.00	11.10	12.30 p.m.	1.15	2.05	4.00
St Pancras	dep.	5.15 a.m.	6.10	7.55	9.05	10.00	11.10	12.30 p.m.	1.15	2.05	4.00
Kentish Town	,,	—	6.14	7.59	9.09	10.04	11.14	—	1.20	2.09	—
Hendon	,,	—	6.37	8.10	9.19	—	—	—	1.39	—	—
Mill Hill	,,	—	6.44	8.16	9.24	—	—	—	1.45	—	—
Elstree	,,	—	6.52	8.23	9.30	—	—	—	1.51	—	—
Radlett	,,	—	6.58	—	9.36	—	—	—	1.57	—	—
St Albans	,,	—	7.07	8.34	9.44	—	11.40	—	2.05	2.36	—
Harpenden	,,	—	7.54	8.46	9.55	—	11.51	—	2.16	2.49	—
Chiltern Green	,,	—	8.00	—	—	—	—	—	2.24	—	—
Luton	,,	—	8.07	8.55	10.04	Slip	12.00	1.09	2.40	2.59	—
Leagrave	,,	—	8.16	—	10.13	—	—	—	2.48	—	—
Harlington	,,	—	8.25	—	10.35	—	12.14	—	2.56	—	—
Flitwick	,,	—	8.32	—	10.42	—	—	—	3.06	—	—
Ampthill	,,	—	8.37	9.16	10.47	—	12.23	—	3.11	3.20	—
Bedford	,,	6.15	9.00	9.32	10.59	11.09	12.38	1.37	3.23	3.38	5.05
Wellingborough	,,	—	9.32	10.00	—	—	1.01	—	—	4.04	—
Kettering	,,	—	—	10.16	—	—	1.16	—	—	4.17	—
Market Harborough	,,	—	—	—	—	—	1.32	2.20	—	—	—
Leicester	arr.	—	—	—	—	12.12	2.02	2.45	—	—	6.07
		A						B			C

continued.

		4.20 p.m.	5.00	5.43	6.05	6.30	8.30	9.15	12.00 midnight
St Pancras	dep.	4.20 p.m.	5.00	5.43	6.05	6.30	8.30	9.15	12.00 midnight
Kentish Town	,,	4.24	5.04	5.48	6.09	6.35	8.34	9.20	12.06 a.m.
Hendon	,,	—	—	—	—	6.54	—	—	—
Mill Hill	,,	—	—	—	—	7.00	—	—	—
Elstree	,,	—	—	—	6.27	7.07	—	—	—
Radlett	,,	—	—	—	6.33	7.14	—	—	—
St Albans	,,	4.51	Slip	6.15	6.41	7.22	9.03	—	12.35
Harpenden	,,	5.01	—	6.26	6.50	7.34	9.12	—	—
Chiltern Green	,,	5.07	—	6.32	—	7.40	—	—	—
Luton	,,	5.13	—	6.38	7.01	7.47	9.22	—	12.51
Leagrave	,,	5.22	—	—	—	7.57	—	—	—
Harlington	,,	5.31	—	6.51	—	8.06	—	—	—
Flitwick	,,	5.38	—	—	—	8.13	—	—	—
Ampthill	,,	5.43	—	7.00	—	8.18	—	—	—
Bedford	,,	5.55	6.07	7.12	7.32	8.30	9.54	10.27	1.20
Wellingborough	,,	—	—	—	7.59	—	10.16	—	—
Kettering	,,	—	—	—	8.20	—	10.30	—	—
Market Harborough	,,	—	—	—	8.38	—	10.47	—	—
Leicester	arr.	—	7.10	—	9.13	—	11.12	11.32	2.26
							D	E	F

Note: A — Newspaper train
B — Matlock and Buxton express
C — Drawing room saloon car in train
D — Mail train
E — Scotch Express
F — Sleeping saloon cars, London to Manchester.
[Note also the importance of Kentish Town as an exchange station. The slip coach services to St Albans and Luton. Harlington (then known as Harlington for Toddington) and Ampthill have a better service than Flitwick.]

B.5 *July 1890 Midland Railway*

Sundays

St Pancras	dep.	7.30 a.m.	9.30	2.30 p.m.	3.15	5.40	8.30	9.15	12.00 midnight
Kentish Town	,,	7.38	9.37	2.34	3.19	5.44	8.34	9.19	12.06 a.m.
Hendon	,,	7.58	9.59	—	—	5.57	—	—	—
Mill Hill	,,	8.07	10.06	—	—	6.04	—	—	—
Elstree	,,	8.15	10.14	—	—	6.12	—	—	—
Radlett	,,	8.21	10.20	—	—	6.18	—	—	—
St Albans	,,	8.30	10.29	3.02	—	6.27	9.03	—	12.35
Harpenden	,,	8.43	10.41	3.11	—	6.39	9.12	—	—
Chiltern Green	,,	8.50	10.48	—	—	6.46	—	—	—
Luton	,,	8.56	10.55	3.20	—	6.52	9.22	—	12.51
Leagrave	,,	9.05	11.04	—	—	7.00	—	—	—
Harlington	,,	9.15	11.14	—	—	7.10	—	—	—
Flitwick	,,	9.22	11.22	—	—	7.17	—	—	—
Ampthill	,,	9.27	11.27	—	—	7.22	—	—	—
Bedford	,,	9.48	11.45	3.52	4.23	7.42	9.54	10.27	1.20
Wellingborough	,,	10.22	—	4.14	—	8.16	10.16	—	—
Kettering	,,	10.45	—	4.29	—	8.38	10.30	—	—
Market Harborough	,,	11.09	—	4.44	—	9.02	10.47	—	—
Leicester	arr.	11.55	—	5.13	5.27	9.47	11.12	11.32	2.26
						A	B	C	D

A — Liverpool & Manchester express
B — Mail
C — Scotch Express; sleeping cars London to Edinburgh & Glasgow
D — Sleeping cars, Liverpool and Manchester.

Sundays

Leicester	dep.				2.46 p.m.		7.32	
Kettering	,,				—	6.25	—	
Wellingborough	,,		—	10.03	—	6.42	—	8.33
Bedford	,,	7.27 a.m.	7.50	10.40	3.52	7.25	8.38	9.00
Ampthill	,,	—	8.03	—	—	—	—	—
Flitwick	,,	—	8.08	—	—	—	—	—
Harlington	,,	—	8.14	—	—	—	—	—
Leagrave	,,	—	8.26	—	—	—	—	—
Luton	,,	—	8.33	11.07	—	—	—	9.26
Chiltern Green	,,	—	8.40	—	—	—	—	—
Harpenden	,,	—	8.46	—	—	—	—	9.38
St Albans	,,	—	8.54	11.25	—	—	—	9.46
Radlett	,,	—	9.04	—	—	—	—	—
Elstree	,,	—	9.10	—	—	—	—	—
Mill Hill	,,	—	9.17	—	—	—	—	—
Hendon	,,	—	9.23	11.47	—	—	—	—
Kentish Town	,,	—	9.42	12.05	4.52	—	9.38	10.12
St Pancras	arr.	8.30	9.50	12.15	5.00	9.35	9.45	10.20
					E			

E — Drawing Room Saloon Cars, Liverpool and Manchester to London.

B.5

July 1890   Midland Railway   Weekdays

Station		1.50 a.m.	7.27	7.03	8.10	7.15	10.42	11.27	A		B
Leicester	dep.	1.50 a.m.				7.15			12.24 p.m.		2.06
Market Harborough	,,	2.14				7.44					
Kettering	,,					8.09		11.27		1.40 p.m.	
Wellingborough	,,	2.40				8.20		11.45		1.50	
Bedford	,,	3.09	7.27	7.03	8.10	8.57	10.42	12.24	1.29 p.m.	2.17	3.10
Ampthill	,,			7.15		9.09		12.37			
Flitwick	,,			7.20		9.14		12.42			
Harlington	,,			7.26		9.21		12.49			
Leagrave	,,			7.38	8.37	9.30		12.58			
Luton	,,			8.00		9.35		1.04		2.42	
Chiltern Green	,,			8.07	8.48			1.13			
Harpenden	,,			8.13	8.57	9.47		1.20		2.54	
St Albans	,,			8.22	9.05	9.59		1.28		3.02	
Radlett	,,			8.30				1.38			
Elstree	,,			8.36	9.17			1.44			
Mill Hill	,,			8.42	9.23			1.51			
Hendon	,,							1.58			
Kentish Town	,,			8.53	9.31	10.22	11.42	2.15	2.28	3.26	4.09
St Pancras	arr.	4.15	8.30	9.00	9.38	10.30	11.50	2.23	2.35	3.35	4.15
									A		B

Continued

Station		4.42	4.08 p.m.	6.40	C	D	7.45
Leicester	dep.	4.42			6.14	7.37	7.45
Market Harborough	,,	5.11					8.30
Kettering	,,	5.35					8.44
Wellingborough	,,	5.45					8.55
Bedford	,,	6.25	4.08 p.m.	6.40	7.18	8.43	9.28
Ampthill	,,		4.20	6.52			9.40
Flitwick	,,		4.25	6.57			
Harlington	,,		4.32	7.04			
Leagrave	,,		4.41	7.13			
Luton	,,	6.55	4.47	7.18	7.44		9.56
Chiltern Green	,,						
Harpenden	,,	7.07					10.08
St Albans	,,	7.15					10.16
Radlett	,,						10.26
Elstree	,,						10.33
Mill Hill	,,						10.40
Hendon	,,						10.46
Kentish Town	,,	7.41					11.04
St Pancras	arr.	7.50			8.25	9.45	11.12
					C	D	

A — Luncheon Saloon Car.
B — Drawing Room Saloon Car, Liverpool to London.
C — Drawing Room Saloon Car, Manchester to London.
D — Dining Saloon Car, Manchester to London.

[Note the excellent service from Bedford; 14 trains to London of which 6 are non-stop.
Harlington is referred to in the timetable as 'Harlington for Toddington'.
Cricklewood and West Hampstead stations are not yet included.
Finchley Road, Haverstock Hill and Camden Road stations were served by the Moorgate Street trains.
Ampthill still had a slightly better service than Flitwick.]

B.6		*May 1872 Midland Railway*			
		Weekdays only			
Bedford	dep.	8.46	9.59	4.12	6.50
Northampton	arr.	9.50	2.10	5.00	9.40
Northampton	dep.	7.10	10.40	2.30	4.50
Bedford	arr.	8.10	11.52	3.31	6.18

[Passengers had to change at Wellingborough in each
direction. This was before the opening of the Bedford &
Northampton Railway.]

B.7		*August 1872 Bedford & Northampton Railway* (worked by the Midland Railway)				
		Weekdays only				
Bedford	dep.	8.40	11.15	1.07	4.17	6.55
Turvey	,,	8.52	11.26	1.19	4.28	7.07
Olney	,,	9.02	11.36	1.29	4.38	7.17
Horton	,,	9.12	—	1.39	—	7.27
Northampton St John's	arr.	9.25	11.55	1.59	4.57	7.40
Northampton St John's	dep.	7.25	10.00	12.45	4.37	6.20
Horton	arr.	7.36	—	12.57	—	6.32
Olney	,,	7.45	10.18	1.07	4.56	6.42
Turvey	,,	7.55	10.27	1.17	5.06	6.52
Bedford	,,	8.07	10.38	1.30	5.17	7.05

[Timetable as advertised in the *Bedfordshire Times*. Midland trains
ran into their own terminus at Northampton. Horton (later
Piddington & Horton) always had a poor service.]

B.8		*July 1890 Midland Railway*			
		Weekdays only			
Bedford	dep.	7.45	12.27	5.05	7.32
Cardington	,,	7.56	12.36	5.13	7.41
Southill	,,	8.05	12.44	5.21	7.49
Shefford	,,	8.11	12.50	5.27	7.55
Henlow	,,	8.23	12.56	5.33	8.03
Hitchin	arr.	8.35	1.07	5.45	8.15
Hitchin	dep.	7.00	9.53	2.56	6.05
Henlow	,,	7.09	10.02	3.05	6.17
Shefford	,,	7.15	10.08	3.10	6.23
Southill	,,	7.21	10.14	3.17	6.29
Cardington	,,	7.29	10.22	3.27	6.37
Bedford	arr.	7.35	10.28	3.33	6.43

B.9   *July 1890*

				Weekdays only		
Northampton	dep.	8.05	9.45	2'15	5.20	7.50
Piddington	,,	8.16	9.56	2.26	5.31	8.01
Olney	,,	8.26	10.06	2.36	5.41	8.11
Turvey	,,	8.35	10.15	2.45	5.50	8.20
Bedford	arr.	8.45	10.25	2.55	6.00	8.30

Bedford	dep.	8.30	11.15	1.25	5.10	7.37
Turvey	,,	8.41	11.26	1.36	5.21	7.48
Olney	,,	8.50	11.35	1.45	5.30	7.57
Piddington	,,	9.00	11.45	1.55	5.40	8.07
Northampton	arr.	9.10	11.55	2.05	5.50	8.17

Appendix C

Timetables for G.N.R. and branches

C.1		*July 1850*
		Eastern Counties Railway
		Weekdays only
London (Shoreditch).	dep.	11.30 a.m.
Cambridge	arr.	1.38 p.m.
Cambridge	dep.	2.00
Huntingdon	arr.	2.55

Huntingdon	dep.	12.40 p.m.
Cambridge	arr.	1.33
Cambridge	dep.	3.06
London (Shoreditch)	arr.	5.20

[The above timetable shows the train service between London and Huntingdon just before the opening of the Great Northern Railway. Huntingdon has been selected so as to show the train services both north and south of the Bedfordshire towns and villages.]

C.2   *July 1860   Great Northern Railway*

Weekdays

Class		1, 2 & 3	1, 2 & 3	1 & 2	1 & 2	1 & 2	1 & 2	1 & 2	1 & 2	1 & 2	1 & 2
King's Cross	dep.	6.30 a.m.	7.40	10.05	12.00	12.25 p.m.	1.45	4.05	5.00	5.05	8.00
Holloway	,,	6.35	—	10.10	—	12.30	—	—	—	—	8.05
Hornsey	,,	6.45	—	10.20	—	12.38	—	4.17	—	—	8.15
Wood Green	,,	6.48	—	—	—	—	—	4.20	—	—	8.18
a Southgate	,,	6.53	—	10.27	—	12.45	—	4.25	—	—	8.23
Barnet	,,	7.00	—	10.35	—	12.52	—	4.33	—	5.25	8.32
Potters Bar	,,	7.09	—	10.43	—	1.01	—	4.42	—	—	8.42
Hatfield	,,	7.20	—	10.53	—	1.13	—	4.52	—	5.40	8.53
Welwyn Junction	,,	—	—	10.58	—	—	—	—	—	5.47	8.58
Welwyn	,,	7.30	—	11.03	—	1.23	2.23	5.00	—	5.52	9.04
Stevenage	,,	7.42	—	11.15	—	1.35	2.35	5.12	—	6.03	9.14
Hitchin	,,	8.00	8.40	11.27	—	1.46	2.50	5.21	—	6.15	9.28
b Arlesey	,,	8.10	—	11.36	—	1.55	3.00	—	—	6.24	9.38
Biggleswade	,,	8.20	—	11.45	—	2.04	3.09	5.34	—	6.32	9.48
c Sandy	,,	8.28	—	11.50	—	2.12	3.17	5.40	—	6.39	9.54
St Neots	,,	8.40	—	12.05	—	2.25	3.30	5.53	—	6.51	10.08
Offord	,,	8.52	—	12.15	—	2.34	3.39	—	—	—	—
Huntingdon	arr.	9.00	9.20	12.25	1.20	2.45	3.50	6.07	6.40	7.04	10.22

Sundays

Class		1, 2 & 3 & Gov.	1, 2 & 3
King's Cross	dep.	7.30 a.m.	8.00 p.m.
Holloway	,,	7.35	—
Hornsey	,,	7.45	8.10
Wood Green	,,	7.48	—
a Southgate	,,	7.53	8.17
Barnet	,,	8.00	8.25
Potters Bar	,,	8.10	8.34
Hatfield	,,	8.22	8.45
Welwyn Junction	,,	8.31	8.50
Welwyn	,,	8.34	8.55
Stevenage	,,	8.40	9.05
Hitchin	,,	9.00	9.20
b Arlesey	,,	9.13	9.32
Biggleswade	,,	9.26	9.42
c Sandy	,,	9.35	9.48
St Neots	,,	9.48	10.02
Offord	,,	10.02	—
Huntingdon	,,	10.13	10.18

FARES from King's Cross.
    Single Journey. To::

	1st	2nd	3rd
Arlesey	7s	5s	3s 1d
Biggleswade	7s 6d	5s 6d	3s 5d
Sandy	8s	6s	3s 8d
St Neots	9s 6d	7s	4s 3½d
Offord	10s	7s	4s 7½d
Huntingdon	10s 6d	8s	4s 10½

[Note: (a) The station is referred to in *Bradshaw* as 'Southgate & Colney Hatch'.
      (b) The station is referred to in *Bradshaw* as 'Arlesey & Shefford Road.'
      (c) The station is referred to in *Bradshaw* as 'Sandy for Bedford'.]

C.2   *July 1860*   *Great Northern Railway*

		Weekdays							*Sundays*
Class		*1 & 2*	*1 & 2*	*1 & 2*	*1 & 2*	*1, 2 & 3*	*1 & 2*	*1 & 2*	*1, 2 & 3*
Huntingdon	dep.	8.43	10.38	1.21	2.28	3.00	6.10	9.04	5.20
Offord	,,	—	10.45	1.29	—	3.06	6.18	—	5.30
St Neots	,,	8.55	10.57	1.40	—	3.15	6.31	9.16	5.45
a Sandy	,,	9.08	11.10	1.52	—	3.27	6.43	9.29	6.00
Biggleswade	,,	9.15	11.20	2.10	—	3.33	6.53	9.36	6.10
b Arlesey	,,	A	11.30	2.20	—	3.41	7.05	9.46	6.22
Hitchin	,,	9.35	11.45	2.35	3.13	4.00	7.25	10.00	6.40
Stevenage	,,	9.43	11.55	—	—	4.10	7.35	10.10	—
Welwyn	,,	9.55	12.10	2.55	—	4.22	7.47	10.20	—
Welwyn Junction	,,	10.00	—	—	—	4.26	7.52	—	—
Hatfield	,,	10.09	12.25	—	—	4.35	8.02	10.30	7.10
Potters Bar	,,	—	—	—	—	4.47	8.13	10.37	—
Barnet	,,	—	—	—	—	4.55	8.23	10.47	—
c Southgate	,,	—	—	—	—	5.05	8.29	10.55	—
Wood Green	,,	—	—	—	—	5.11	8.34	—	—
Hornsey	,,	—	—	—	—	5.15	8.40	11.00	—
Holloway	,,	—	—	3.35	—	5.25	8.55	11.10	7.40
King's Cross	arr.	10.40	1.00	3.40	4.00	5.30	9.00	11.15	7.45

Note: A — stops to set down passengers only.
      a — In *Bradshaw* 'Sandy for Bedford'.
      b — In *Bradshaw* 'Arlesey & Shefford Road'.
      c — In *Bradshaw* 'Southgate & Colney Hatch'.

[Note also the poor service for 3rd class passengers.
   Tempsford station not opened until 1862.
   Arlesey Siding station not opened until 1866 and renamed Three Counties twenty years after.
   There is no mention in 1860 of Knebworth, Brookmans Park, Hadley Wood, Oakleigh Park,
Harringay and Finsbury Park stations.]

J

C.3 *July 1890 Great Northern Railway*

Weekdays

		5.25 a.m.	7.45	8.45	10.32	11.45	1.25 p.m.	3.00	4.20	5.00	5.30
King's Cross	dep.	5.25 a.m.	7.45	8.45	10.32	11.45	1.25 p.m.	3.00	4.20	5.00	5.30
Finsbury Park	,,	5.30	7.54	8.51	10.45	11.51	1.35	—	4.27	—	—
Hatfield	,,	5.52	8.23	9.15	11.17	12.16	2.02	—	4.53	5.25	—
Welwyn	,,	—	—	—	11.25	—	2.10	—	—	—	—
Knebworth	,,	—	—	—	11.31	—	2.17	—	—	—	—
Stevenage	,,	—	—	—	11.39	—	2.24	—	—	—	—
Hitchin	,,	6.15	8.52	9.35	11.48	12.39	2.41	3.44	5.16	5.48	—
Three Counties	,,	6.25	8.59	—	11.56	—	2.48	—	—	5.55	—
Arlesey	,,	6.29	9.02	—	12.00	—	2.51	—	—	5.58	—
Biggleswade	,,	6.39	9.11	—	12.09	—	3.00	—	5.30	6.07	—
Sandy Junction	,,	6.47	9.18	—	12.18	12.55	3.07	—	5.37	6.13	—
Tempsford	,,	6.55	9.24	—	12.24	—	3.13	—	—	6.30	—
St Neots	,,	7.05	9.32	—	12.33	—	3.21	—	5.49	6.38	—
Offord	,,	7.15	9.39	—	12.41	—	3.29	—	—	6.44	—
Huntingdon	arr.	7.26	9.46	10.06	12.49	1.14	3.36	—	6.03	6.50	Slip

		Weekdays continued			*Sundays*	
King's Cross	dep.	5.50 p.m.	7.00	9.35	8.35 a.m.	6.30 p.m.
Finsbury Park	,,	5.57	7.07	9.42	8.46	6.40
Hatfield	,,	6.22	7.30	10.04	9.36	7.24
Welwyn	,,	6.30	—	—	9.47	7.33
Knebworth	,,	6.36	—	—	9.54	—
Stevenage	,,	6.42	7.46	—	10.00	7.45
Hitchin	,,	6.51	7.54	10.27	10.10	7.56
Three Counties	,,	6.58	8.01	10.34	10.17	8.03
Arlesey	,,	7.01	8.04	10.37	10.20	8.06
Biggleswade	,,	7.10	8.13	10.46	10.29	8.15
Sandy Junction	,,	7.16	8.19	10.52	10.38	8.22
Tempsford	,,	7.22	8.25	—	10.45	—
St Neots	,,	7.30	8.33	11.04	10.55	8.34
Offord	,,	7.36	8.40	—	11.03	—
Huntingdon	arr.	7.45	8.48	11.16	11.12	8.47

[Note: Huntingdon is served by one Slip Coach from the 5.30 p.m.]

FARES

From King's Cross to:	Single 1st	2nd	3rd	Return 1st	2nd	3rd
Three Counties	5s 6d	4s 3d	2s 11½d	11s	8s 6d	5s 11d
Arlesey and Shefford Road	6s	4s 3d	3s 1d	11s 9d	8s 6d	6s 2d
Biggleswade	6s 6d	4s 9d	3s 5d	12s 6d	9s 3d	6s 10d
Sandy	7s	5s	3s 8d	13s 6d	10s	7s 4d
Tempsford	7s 6d	5s 6d	3s 11d	14s 3d	11s	7s 10d

First, Second and Third Class coaches now on all trains.

C.3   *July 1890*   *Great Northern Railway*

Weekdays

Huntingdon	dep.	8.02 a.m.	9.45	10.54	1.25 p.m.	2.42	4.46	6.30	7.23	7.42	10.29
Offord	,,	8.08	—	11.00	1.31	2.48	4.52	—	—	7.48	—
St Neots	,,	8.15	9.56	11.07	1.39	2.55	4.59	—	7.34	7.58	10.41
Tempsford	,,	8.23	—	11.15	1.46	3.03	5.08	—	—	8.03	—
a Sandy Junction	,,	8.34	10.08	11.22	1.53	3.10	5.42	—	7.50	8.10	10.53
Biggleswade	,,	8.41	10.14	11.28	2.00	3.17	5.49	—	7.57	8.17	10.59
b Arlesey	,,	8.48	—	11.35	2.07	3.24	6.08	—	8.04	8.24	—
Three Counties	,,	8.52	—	11.38	2.10	3.27	6.12	—	8.08	8.28	—
Hitchin	,,	8.58	—	11.44	2.17	3.34	6.19	7.03	8.15	8.35	11.12
Stevenage	,,	—	—	11.55	3.03	3.56	—	—	—	8.53	—
Knebworth	,,	—	—	12.01	3.10	4.02	—	—	—	8.59	—
Welwyn	,,	—	—	12.08	3.17	4.09	—	—	—	9.06	—
Hatfield	,,	—	—	12.17	3.26	4.17	6.45	—	8.45	9.15	—
Finsbury Park	,,	9.44	11.04	12.29	3.55	4.39	7.18	—	9.06	9.49	11.54
King's Cross	arr.	9.50	11.10	12.45	4.00	4.45	7.23	7.45	9.13	9.55	12.00

Sundays

Huntingdon	dep.	5.40	8.47
Offord	,,	5.46	—
St Neots	,,	5.53	—
Tempsford	,,	6.02	—
a Sandy Junction	,,	6.10	—
Biggleswade	,,	6.17	—
b Arlesey	,,	6.25	—
Three Counties	,,	6.30	—
Hitchin	,,	6.38	9.20
Stevenage	,,	—	—
Knebworth	,,	—	—
Welwyn	,,	—	—
Hatfield	,,	7.11	—
Finsbury Park	,,	7.36	10.04
King's Cross	arr.	7.50	10.10

[Note: a. Sandy for Bedford now called Sandy Junction in *Bradshaw*
b full name of station—Arlesey and Shefford Road.]

C.4 *July 1890   Great Northern Railway*

		Weekdays									
Dunstable (L.N.W.)	dep.	6.00 a.m.	7.10	8.12	8.20	9.25	10.12	10.45	12.45 p.m.	2.05	3.35
Dunstable Church Street	,,	6.05	7.15	8.16	8.28	9.30	10.17	10.50	12.50	2.10	3.40
Luton	,,	6.15	7.32	8.25	8.40	9.40	10.32	11.40	1.07	2.20	3.35
New Mill End	,,	—	7.39	—	8.47	—	10.39	11.47	1.14		4.00
Harpenden	,,		7.44		8.52		10.44	11.52	1.19		4.05
Wheathampstead	,,		7.49		8.57		10.49	11.57	1.24		4.10
Ayot	,,		7.55		9.03		10.55	12.04	1.31		4.16
Hatfield	arr.		8.05		9.12		11.04	12.12	1.40		4.25

		Sundays									
Dunstable (L.N.W.)	dep.	5.05 p.m.	5.50	7.32	7.42	8.31	9.55	—	—	—	
Dunstable Church Street	,,	5.10	5.55	7.37	7.50	8.35	10.00	8.05 a.m.	10.50	5.55	8.35
Luton	,,	5.30	6.05	7.47	8.07	8.45	10.10	8.15	11.00	6.05	8.45
New Mill End	,,	5.37	—	—	8.14	—	—	8.23	—	6.13	—
Harpenden	,,	5.42			8.19			8.28		6.18	
Wheathampstead	,,	5.47			8.24			8.33		6.23	
Ayot	,,	5.53			8.30			8.39		6.29	
Hatfield	arr.	6.02			8.39			8.50		6.40	

[Note: New Mill End renamed Luton Hoo in 1892.]

		Weekdays									
Hatfield	dep.			8.25	9.57				12.20		3.18
Ayot	,,			8.35	10.06				12.29		3.27
Wheathampstead	,,			8.41	10.12				12.35		3.33
Harpenden	,,			8.53	10.17				12.40		3.38
New Mill End	,,			8.58	10.22				12.45		3.43
Luton	,,	6.45 a.m.	7.50	8.40	9.09	10.30	11.08	12.20 p.m.	1.02	2.45	4.00
Dunstable Church St.	,,	6.56	8.00	8.50	9.19	10.40	11.18	12.30	1.12	2.55	4.11
Dunstable (L.N.W.)	arr.	7.00	8.05	8.55	9.24	10.44	11.22	12.35	1.16	2.59	4.16

Hatfield	dep.	4.53		6.26		7.33		10.10
Ayot	,,	5.03		6.36		7.43		10.20
Wheathampstead	,,	5.09		6.42		7.49		10.26
Harpenden	,,	5.14		6.47		7.54		10.31
New Mill End	,,	5.19		6.52		7.59		10.36
Luton	,,	5.29	6.30	7.04	8.00	8.10	9.23	10.47
Dunstable Church Street	,,	5.39	6.40	7.14	8.10	8.20	9.33	10.58
Dunstable (L.N.W.)	arr.	5.45	6.50	7.19	8.15	8.25	9.38	11.02

		Sundays			
Hatfield	dep.		9.42		7.20
Ayot	,,		9.52		7.40
Wheathampstead	,,		9.58		7.47
Harpenden	,,		10.03		7.52
New Mill End	,,		10.08		7.57
Luton	,,	7.35 a.m.	10.25	5.25 p.m.	8.10
Dunstable Church Street	,,	7.45	10.35	5.35	8.20
Dunstable (L.N.W.)	arr.	—			—

C.5 *Sandy & Potton Railway July 1860 Weekdays*

The Sandy & Potton Railway appeared in *Bradshaw* probably from January 1858, the last entry being in December 1861. Instead of the usual tables the services were mentioned in a paragraph in the corner of the page applying to the Great Northern Railway main line. The following is to be found on page 68 of the *Bradshaw* for July 1860.

POTTON & SANDY

From Potton at 8.10 and 10.50 morning; 3 and 6.20 afternoon.
From Sandy at 9.10 and 11.55 morning; 3.30 and 6.55 afternoon.
Distance 3 miles; Time on journey—10 minutes
Fares Potton-Sandy: First class 9d; second class 6d; third class 3d.
Day tickets 1s 9d.
Fares to London First class 8s 9d; second class 6s 6d; third class 3s 11d.
Day tickets to London First class 13s; second class 9s 9d.

There is no mention of Sunday services.

The following table has been prepared to show connecting trains.

S. & P.R.					
Potton	dep.	8.10 a.m.	10.50	3.00 p.m.	6.20
Sandy	arr.	8.20	11.00	3.10	6.30
G.N.R.					
Sandy	dep.	9.08	11.10	3.27	6.43
King's Cross	arr.	10.40	1.00 p.m.	5.30	9.00
Class		*1 & 2*	*1, 2 & 3*	*1, 2 & 3*	*1 & 2*

S. & P.R.					
Potton	dep.	8.10 a.m.	10.50	3.00 p.m.	6.20
Sandy	arr.	8.20	11.00	3.10	6.30
G.N.R.					
Sandy	dep.	8.28	11.50	3.17	6.39
Huntingdon	,,	9.00	12.25	3.50	7.04
Peterborough	,,	9.40	2.15 p.m.	4.30	7.35
Grantham	arr.	—	3.20	5.45	8.33
Class		*1, 2 & 3*	*1 & 2*	*1 & 2*	*1 & 2*

G.N.R.					
Class		*1 & 2*	*1, 2 & 3*	*1, 2 & 3*	*1 & 2*
Grantham	dep.	7.15 a.m.	8.50	—	4.15 p.m.
Peterborough	,,	8.10	10.05	—	5.35
Huntingdon	,,	8.43	10.38	3.00 p.m.	6.10
Sandy	,,	9.08	11.10	3.27	6.43
S. & P. R.					
Sandy	,,	9.10	11.55	3.30	6.55
Potton	arr.	9.20	12.05	3.40	7.05

G.N.R.					
Class		*1, 2 & 3*	*1 & 2*	*1 & 2*	*1 & 2*
King's Cross	dep.	6.30 a.m.	10.05	1.45 p.m.	5.05
Sandy	,,	8.28	11.50	3.17	6.39
S. & P.R.					
Sandy	dep.	9.10	11.55	3.30	6.55
Potton	arr.	9.20	12.05	3.40	7.05

Appendix D

Railways in Bedfordshire for which Plans were deposited, but which were never built

Year	Names	Length		Reason
1844	Ely & Bedford	44	miles	withdrawn
,,	Eastern Counties, extension to Hertford and Biggleswade	10	,,	Rejected Standing Orders
,,	Direct Northern, first route	177	,,	Amalgamated with London & York to become G.N.R.
,,	London & York	186	,,	See above
1845	Great Northern Railway extension to Luton and Dunstable	19	,,	Hatfield-St Albans passed; rest deferred to 1860
.,	Leicester & Bedford	63½	,,	Rejected in Lords
,,	Northampton Bedford & Cambridge	20¼	,,	Wound up
,,	Wolverton Newport Pagnell & Bedford	11	,,	Withdrawn
,,	Ely & Huntingdon, extension to Bedford	20½	,,	Withdrawn
,,	London & Nottingham	69	,,	Wound up
,,	Cambridge & Oxford	73	,,	Royston-Hitchin 18 miles, built
	South Midland Railway	46	,,	Rejected by House of Commons
,,	Midland & Eastern Counties	53	,,	Wound up
,,	Direct London & Manchester	175	,,	Wound up
,,	Bedford & Cambridge	26½	,,	Defeated Standing Orders
,,	Bedfordshire, Hertfordshire & Essex	55	,,	Abandoned
,,	Eastern Counties Railway, extension to Bedford from Cambridge (Shelford)	27½	,,	Powers lapsed
,,	Eastern Counties Railway, extension to Huntingdon and Bedford	44	,,	Rejecetd by Parliament
	Direct Northern Railway, second route	177	,,	Amalg. with Ldn & York to form Great Northern
,,	London & Birmingham extension to Luton, Watford and Dunstable	20	,,	Withdrawn
1846	Midland extension to Hitchin	63	,,	Act obtained but deferred
1852	Great Northern, Bedford branch	8	,,	Act obtained but postponed
1858	Bedford, Potton & Cambridge	29	,,	Rejected by Commons
1860	St Albans & Shefford	24	,,	Abandoned
1864	East & West Junction extension to Bedford	26	,,	Bankrupt
,,	Bedford, Northampton & Leamington	47	,,	Abandoned
1865	East & West Junction extension to Hitchin	38	,,	Bankrupt
1871	Towcester & Hitchin	37	,,	Abandoned
1885	Bedford & Peterborough	31	,,	Withdrawn
1910	Leagrave & Luton Light Railway	1½	mile	Unable to comply with Luton R.D.C.

Appendix E

Excursions

Midland Railway

Horticultural and Floral Fete and Balloon Ascent at Wellingborough
On Tuesday, 11th September, 1860 a special train will leave Hitchin, Bedford and the undermentioned stations for Wellingborough.

Fares there and back and Times of Starting

Hitchin	10.30 a.m.	1s 6d
Henlow	10.40	1s 6d
Shefford	10.47	1s 6d
Southill	10.57	1s 6d
Cardington	11.08	1s
Bedford	11.15	1s
Oakley	11.25	1s
Sharnbrook	11.35	9d

Children under 3, free; above 3 and under 12, half fares
Tickets not transferable.
The special train will leave Wellingborough in returning at 6.30 the same day.
Tickets will be available to return by this train only.

James Allport, *Derby*

Great Northern Railway

International Exhibition   29th July 1862

Huntingdon	dep.	5.40 a.m.
St Neots	,,	6.00
Sandy	,,	6.20
Biggleswade	,,	6.30
King's Cross	arr.	8.15

Fare 3s.   Return train 7.20 p.m.

Seymour Clarke

Midland Railway

International Exhibition

			Fare			Covered carriage		
Leicester	dep.	4.15 a.m.		1st class	9s	Covered carriage		4s 6d
Kettering	,,	5.32	,,	,,	8s	,,	,,	4s
Bedford	,,	6.30	,,	,,	6s	,,	,,	2s 6d
Shefford	,,	6.52	,,	,,	6s	,,	,,	2s 6d
King's Cross	arr.	8.40						

Return at 8.30

James Allport, *General Manager*

Midland Railway

Kingsbury and Hendon Summer Races
Thursday 23rd July 1868
A cheap excursion train will run to Hendon by the Midland Railway's new route as under:

			Fare			Covered carriage		
Bedford	dep.	10.00 a.m.		1st class	5s	Covered carriage		2s 6d
Ampthill	,,	10.16	,,	,,	5s	,,	,,	2s 6d
Harlington	,,	10.27	,,	,,	4s	,,	,,	2s
Leagrave	,,	10.39	,,	,,	4s	,,	,,	2s

Children under 3, free; above 3 and under 12, half fare.
Tickets not transferable. No luggage allowed.
The return train will leave Hendon at 7.15 p.m. the same day and the tickets will be available for return by this train only.

James Allport, *General Manager*

Great Northern Railway   *Cheap Day Trip to the Seaside*
Monday 10th August 1868
A cheap excursion will run to Ramsgate, Margate and Broadstairs as under:

			Fare			Covered carriage		
Huntingdon	dep.	5.33 a.m.		1st Class	12s	Covered carriage		6s
Offord	,,	5.41	,,	,,	12s	,,	,,	6s
St Neots	,,	5.50	,,	,,	12s	,,	,,	6s
Tempsford	,,	5.58	,,	,,	12s	,,	,,	6s
Sandy	,,	6.07	,,	,,	12s	,,	,,	6s
Biggleswade	,,	6.14	,,	,,	11s	,,	,,	5s 6d
Arlesey	,,	6.23	,,	,,	11s	,,	,,	5s 6d
Arlesey Siding	,,	6.27	,,	,,	11s	,,	,,	5s 6d
Hitchin	,,	6.40	,,	,,	10s	,	,,	5s
Margate	arr.	10.15						
Broadstairs	,,	10.25						
Ramsgate	,,	10.30						

Return from Ramsgate at 6.45, Broadstairs 6.50 and Margate 6.55, same day only.

Seymour Clarke, *General Manager*

Appendix F
Railway Accidents
Extracts from the Coroner's Inquest Book for Bedfordshire, 1854–86

Extracts from the Coroner's Inquest Book for Bedfordshire, 1854-86				
Date	Name	Place	Cause	Age
24th February 1854	Thomas Haining	Biggleswade	Knocked down by train	21
27th December 1856	Richard Street	Souldrop	(navvy)	26
24th May 1860	W. S. Clarke	Biggleswade	Standing on top of engine and striking a bridge	24
19th March 1861	James Cherry	Stratford	Run over	37
5th December 1861	Alf. Eddington	Biggleswade	Jumped out of carriage	28
10th July 1862	Wm. Hatton	Shefford	Run over	62
4th October 1862	John York	Biggleswade	Knocked down	47
17th January 1866	Charles Bell	Luton	Navvy in Ampthill tunnel: run over	22
1st September 1868	H. Darnell	Sharnbrook	Run over	65
17th October 1868	J. Rainbow	Biggleswade	,, ,,	41
14th May 1869	Joseph Dixey	Sandy	,, ,,	75
14th June 1870	Thomas Baston	Biggleswade	,, ,,	32
	Kim Larman	,,	,, ,,	30
8th August 1870	Mary Roberts	Luton	,, ,,	74
22nd September 1870	Fred Howkins	Arlesey	,, ,,	28
22nd May 1871	David Winch	East Hyde	,, ,,	22
17th October 1871	Robert Barcock	Sharnbrook	Crushed between wagons	40
3rd August 1872	Silas Smith	Chiltern Green	Run over	30
10th December 1872	Georgina Smith	Sharnbrook	,, ,,	21
30th April 1873	Jonathan Dunt	Luton	,, ,,	46
17th September 1873	Geo. Kefford	Tempsford	,, ,,	11
7th March 1874	Wm. Bosworth	Turvey	,, ,,	40
12th October 1874	Benj. Watson	Luton	,, ,,	26
2nd December 1874	Jas. Wagstaff	Biggleswade	Fell from platform	64
11th March 1875	Wm. Edwards	Sharnbrook	Run over	47
25th March 1875	James Barnet	Luton	Jumped from train	31
10th July 1875	Benj. White	Moggerhanger	Run over	49
23rd December 1876	Thos. Pepper	Arlesey Siding	Collision	49
	John Lovell	,, ,,	,,	25
,,	Maurice Mitchell	,, ,,	,,	21
,,	Lucy Thompson	,, ,,	,,	34
	Abergail Longstaff	,, ,,	,,	29
30th September 1880	George Rose	Totternhoe	Struck by wagon	8
1st April 1881	Benjamin Franklin	Luton	Run over	21
	Thomas Hawkins	,,	,, ,,	22
15th June 1882	William Clarke	Wymington	Killed by fall of earth	34
12th December 1882	Joseph White	Sharnbrook	Run over	40
27th March 1883	Mary Ann Gardner	Luton	,, ,,	26
7th July 1883	Charles Truett	Sharnbrook	,, ,,	54
4th August 1883	James Smith	Souldrop	,, ,,	53
6th November 1883	Jas. Partridge	Wymington	,, ,,	26
25th June 1884	James Pratt	Biggleswade	,, ,,	44
3rd October 1885	Wm. Baldwin	Sandy	,, ,,	13
11th January 1886	F. O. Tofield	Luton	,, ,,	17
14th January 1886	Albert Bunker	Oakley	Run over	16
9th June 1886	George Barley	Sharnbrook	,, ,,	55
5th November 1886	A. L. Graham	,,	Fell from train	56

Appendix G

Summary of Bedfordshire lines

London & Birmingham Railway
Engineer:	Robert Stephenson
Contractors:	Grissell & Peto (Buildings at Euston and much of the track)
	- Pritchard (Weedon contract)
	J. Nowell (Kilsby tunnel)
	R. Diggle (Birmingham district)
	J. Bramah (Buildings at Curzon Street, Birmingham)
	and others
Act:	1833
Opening:	17th September 1838 (throughout)
Note:	Name changed to London & North Western Railway in 1846 after amalgamation with the Grand Junction Railway and others.

Bedford & London & Birmingham Railway
Engineer:	Robert Stephenson
Contractor:	T. Jackson
Act:	1845
Opened:	17th November 1846
Note:	Absorbed by the L.N.W.R.

Dunstable Railway
Engineer:	Robert Stephenson
Contractors:	London & Birmingham Railway
Act:	1845
Opened:	1st June 1848
Closed:	2nd July 1962
Note:	Chairman—George Stephenson; a director Richard Gutteridge Absorbed by the L.N.W.R.

Great Northern Railway
Engineer:	William Cubitt
Contractor:	Thomas Brassey
Act:	1846
Opened:	8th August 1850
Note:	Original terminus Maiden Lane, London. King's Cross opened 1852. Direct line through Newark opened 1st August 1852.

Midland Railway
Extension from Leicester (Wigston Junction) to Hitchin
Engineer:	Charles Liddell
Contractor:	Thomas Brassey
Act:	1855
Opened:	8th May 1857
Note:	Reduced from main line to branch status on 13th July 1868
Closed:	1st January 1962.

Midland Railway
Extension from Bedford to St Pancras
Engineers:	Liddell & Barlow
Contractors:	Thomas Brassey, A .Ritson, Waring Bros and others
Act:	1863
Opened:	To Moorgate Street 13th July 1868; to St Pancras 1st October 1868
Note:	Tracks quadrupled from 1880

Luton Dunstable & Welwyn Junction Railway
Engineer:	J. C. Birkinshaw
Contractors:	Jackson & Bean
Act:	1856
Opened:	Dunstable to Luton 3rd May 1858; Luton to Welwyn Junction 1st September 1860
Closed:	April 1965
Note:	The section opened in 1860 was under the name of the Hertford Luton & Dunstable Railway.

Sandy & Potton Railway
Engineer: Brundell (of Doncaster)
Contractor: Culshaw (of Biggleswade)
Act: None required
Opened: 9th November 1857
Note: Absorbed by the Bedford & Cambridge Railway 1862. The locomotive 'Shannon' has
                  been fully restored to working order.

Bedford & Cambridge Railway
Engineer: (1) L. A. Gordon
                  (2) Charles Liddell
Contractor: Joseph Firbank
Act: 1860
Opened: 7th July 1862
Closed: 1st January 1968.

Bedford & Northampton Railway
Engineer: Charles Liddell
Contractors: Clark & Punchard
Act: 1856
Opened: 1t1h June 1872
Closed: 31st March 1962.

INDEX OF NAMES

INDEX OF SUBJECTS